THE MAGIC HUNDRED

THE MAGIC HUNDRED

How To Go From Serial Goal-SETTING
To Serious Goal-GETTING
In Just 100 Days

DAX MOY

authorHOUSE®

AuthorHouse™
1663 Liberty Drive
Bloomington, IN 47403
www.authorhouse.com
Phone: 1-800-839-8640

Published by AuthorHouse   07/17/2012

ISBN: 978-1-4259-8496-0 (sc)

Any people depicted in stock imagery provided by Thinkstock are models, and such images are being used for illustrative purposes only.
Certain stock imagery © Thinkstock.

Because of the dynamic nature of the Internet, any web addresses or links contained in this book may have changed since publication and may no longer be valid. The views expressed in this work are solely those of the author and do not necessarily reflect the views of the publisher, and the publisher hereby disclaims any responsibility for them.

For my brother Kaz, who left us
unexpectedly without ever seeing
his own list finished.

Don't worry bro' I'll finish it for you . . .

Table of Contents   Page

Thank You's

Writing a book of any kind is a huge undertaking and one that is virtually impossible to accomplish alone. In fact, those that say they did are doing a huge disservice to the people in their lives who gave them support, encouragement or even just the 'space' to do what they need to do.

In my case, I would particularly like to thank my beautiful, wonderful, amazing wife Deana for her unwavering support and persistent encouragement as well as the faith in me that I would achieve what I set out to do.

There were many evenings when she and my children Kayleigh, Reece, Sara and Connor barely saw me (or saw only the back of my head) while I sat at my computer researching and writing my 'little book'.

Many evenings!

Without her care and understanding, this book and the audio programme would simply not have come to reality. So, to Deana and my lovely kids, I'd like to say 'thankyou' from the bottom of my heart. I love you all so much.

Also, a big thankyou to my mum, Teresa, whose care, support and belief in me has been an incessant cornerstone of my life. Thanks mum!

I'd also like to say thankyou to my mentors Bob Proctor and Joe Vitale whose examples of what you can achieve with a clear and definite goal and the persistence and dedication to achieving it.

Finally, I'd like to say thank you to the thousands of people who have already been practising the principles taught throughout the first edition of this book. Literally thousands of people from all around the world have provided the feedback that has made this new and revised edition possible.

I owe you all so much.

Thankyou with all my heart

Dax

Thank YOU For Coming!

Seriously, thank you for coming. Thank you for choosing to be right here in this place right now.

I realise there are literally thousands of other things you could be doing right now instead of reading this but somehow you've ended up here with me for which I'm profoundly thankful and honoured as well as genuinely pleased as I know you're going to get a lot from our time together.

I have no idea what brought you to be holding this book in your hands at this particular moment in time. I've no idea of what you want or why you want it and, I promise, I'm certainly not going to try and tell you these things. Your goals always have been and always will be your own, not just extensions of mine.

But I *am* going make it my business to help you discover how to get them into your life in the fastest time possible and with the least effort.

In fact, you could say that this book has arrived in your life at exactly the right moment. The perfect moment. You may not recognise or even believe that right now but you will by the time you finish reading.

For now, let me just say that if you've been searching for a way to get more of what you from life faster than ever before and with less fuss and less hassle then you've found it. I believe that 100%, it's not just marketing hype. After all, if you're reading this then you've already bought the program so there's no need for me to sell you on this is there?

You WILL achieve some pretty dramatic things over the next 100 days . . . if you actually apply what I'm sharing with you.

But I need to warn you advance . . .

If you're looking for a softly-softly, sit back, think happy thoughts 'believe it and it's yours' kind of approach then you may be in for a bit of shock. This isn't one of those books that promises that all you have to do is think intensely about what you want and the cosmic ordering service or law of attraction will deliver it to you.

They can't and they won't.

This is a program of action-oriented goal achievement. Nothing more, nothing less. If you're happy with that then read on, if not, if you'd rather take the passive *think it and it's yours* route then you may be better off sending the book back to wherever you bought it for a refund.
I'm pretty sure that won't happen though.

First, because for whatever reason this book has ended up in your hands. You were *meant* to be reading it right now at this very moment and, if you were meant to read it then it's right for you.

Second, because the principles I'm sharing in this book work for everyone every time. What's not to like?

So dive into this book. Devour it cover to cover. Read every page as many times as it takes to truly 'get' what's being said and then, without delay, start taking action on what you've learned.

Think of it like a 100 day experiment with you and your life as the test subjects and make sure you get into the lab every single day for a hundred days and see what you come up with.

Think on it this way. Whether you take action or not, those hundred days are going to pass *anyway.* You can choose to sit back and passively watch as they fly by or you can actively participate in them and see just how much influence you really have in shaping and moulding them to your dreams.

The choice is yours.

It's a bit like that scene from the move *The Matrix* where Neo has the choice to take either the red pill or the blue pill. The red pill reveals the truth but will change his world forever and the blue pill keeps everything just as it right now.

In the movie Neo picks red.

What about you?

Now, I don't have any pills for you but my red pill equivalent is to turn the page. Blue is to stop reading.

Your choice.

See you after you decide . . . or not!

Truth, joy and love

Dax

YOU CHOSE RED . . . THANK YOU!

(You Won't Regret It)

Introduction

Before you start reading about The MAGIC Hundred and setting about creating your very own 100 day goal achievement strategy, I want to take the pretty unusual step of telling what this book *isn't*, that way you won't start the program with a head full of preconceived ideas about what you're letting yourself in for and, in doing so, scupper your chances of real success before you even get started.

For a start, this isn't a book of interesting theories, good ideas or neat concepts to be read and then left to gather dust on your bookshelf as soon as you're done reading.

Likewise, it's not a book full of so-called 'secrets' and it's not a book full of well meaning, yet totally useless blather that will claim to know the specific circumstances of your life and how to use the secrets of the universe to fix all your problems.

It's none of these things.

In fact, despite what you may have thought when you picked this book up, this is not even a book about goal-setting!

You see, the truth is, there are already more than enough books out there that teach the process of setting goals and so writing yet another one is simply unnecessary and, well, superfluous.

No, The MAGIC Hundred is none of these things.

And yet . . .

As you read through the following pages you WILL learn the truth about goals, what they really are, where their power lies, how to set them so that motivate, inspire and scare you and, most important of all, how to actually *achieve* them so that rather than being one of the multitude of goal *setters,* you can finally take your rightful place amongst those who actually have become goal *getters.*

(There's a VAST difference!)

In fact, if you follow the program exactly as I've laid it out within this book, I absolutely guarantee you that it'll deliver more positive results into your life than probably ANYTHING you've ever tried before!

When I say MORE I *mean* more!

More focus . . .

More clarity . . .

More passion . . .

More results . . .

More . . . well . . . more happiness!

This system is amazingly powerful (as you'll see shortly) yet so simple that ANYONE can use it and get results from it faster than you'd ever believe possible and with less fuss, less worry and less disappointment that most other systems you've tried before.

You know the ones I'm talking about.

Those systems that promise you that if you focus on something, think positive thoughts and then focus on it some more that the very goals you're hoping to achieve will somehow materialise right before your very eyes.

We all know that's not true.

We know before we even begin setting our goals this way that they're doomed to failure yet still we continue hoping against hope that 'this time' it'll work.

This reminds me of my favourite definition of insanity . . . continuously doing the same things yet experiencing a different result.

By this definition, I've got to tell you, most people are certifiably INSANE!

Well, we're going to stop this madness starting today.

We're going to break this ongoing cycle of insanity and try something completely different, something that we've never tried before.

We're going to break the cycle of failure and make ourselves winners, successful people EVERY SINGLE DAY for the next 100 days.

We're going to embark upon a quest to both set and, more importantly, *achieve* a series of goals that, if acted upon exactly as I'm going to be sharing with you throughout this book for the next 100 days, NOT kinda, NOT sorta, NOT maybe but EXACTLY, will change your life in so many ways that I can't even begin to describe.

And the best bit is, it won't even feel like a struggle.

For a 100 days it'll feel like you're freewheeling downhill, and that you're doing things and achieving things with far less effort than before.

You'll have more motivation to achieve your goals, more desire to take positive action and, as a consequence, more results than you'd ever believe possible.

Now, that's not to say that it'll ALL be easy.

It won't be.

Getting started on the magic hundred takes inspiration, motivation and dedication and, truth be told, a little perspiration too, or at least a little effort, in order to lift your ideas off of the ground.

But once they are your life is going to change . . . and fast!

For my part, I'm going to make sure that you get all the information you need to turn your goals into reality. I'll tell you everything you need to know and I'll support you every step of the way whilst you're getting there.

But I can't do it for you.

Only you can do that.

So for your part, you need to enter this MAGIC Hundred challenge with the mindset of someone who's committed to following through on the promises you'll be making to yourself over the next hundred days. Do that and your success is guaranteed.

Let's get started shall we?

Why You Need To Stop Using Your Story As An Excuse For Not Having What You Want

This section wasn't in the original program. I wasn't confident enough of who I was in relation to my readers to share what I'm about to share in the following pages. I thought that they'd judge me and think less of me because of it.

Now I don't care.

The story doesn't define me.

It doesn't tell you who I am, who I want to be or who I'm going to end up becoming. It just tells you who I was at one point in my life and points to some of the choices and changes I've made along the way that have led me to writing this book.

Nothing more, nothing less.

Well, that's not entirely true. If it were then I wouldn't have included it this time around.

The truth is, I want the story to illustrate to you that regardless of where you're at right now, where you've been in the past or what's happened to you along the way that you are not 'doomed' as many people think, to playing out the role that's been assigned to you by others.

You have the ability to choose each and every day of your life what role you wish to play, how you want to play it and for how long.

I know it doesn't seem that way sometimes but it's true.

See for yourself . . .

Let me set the story for you . . . .

I grew up on several of Central London's housing estates that had been built and reserved for the poorest of London's residents and where practically every family was either legitimately on welfare due to genuine financial hardship, or else conning the welfare system by making claims whilst working for cash and avoiding taxes.

The areas I lived in were high in poverty, high in crime, high in violence and high in alcohol abuse and low in just about anything that could even remotely come close to the kind of life that anyone would ever call satisfying, let alone successful.

And that was true of my home too.

My mother genuinely loved her three sons, of which I was the oldest, and tried her hardest to make sure that there was always food on the table and that we were always clean, well dressed and well cared for but struggled against the fact money was scarce and that what little there was, was often taken for booze by my alcoholic stepfather who would disappear for days at a time on drink binges leaving us with cornflakes and little else and return, more often than not, in violent rages where he would beat my mother, us kids or both.

So we spent a lot of our free time playing outside in the streets so that we could make believe and pretend that what was happening at home wasn't and that life was better than it really was.

My brother Kaz and I would often resort to stealing milk and bread off of other people's doorsteps on the way to school and call it breakfast and then line up for seconds of our free school lunches to make sure we got enough to eat as well as resorting to the occasional shoplifting whenever the opportunity to grab a chocolate bar or packet of cookies presented itself.

Looking back, my brother and I became pretty feral in many respects, dealing with bullies at school who would pick on us because of our many times repaired hand-me-down clothing as well as the bullies on the housing estates who would want to take from us what little we had for no other reason than the fact that they wanted it.

By necessity we learned to take care of ourselves pretty well and, though we always did our best to keep ourselves to ourselves, found that we had to fight almost every day whether at school, at home or on the journey in between.

As our childhood years passed us by nothing about our lives really changed. There were still drunken arguments and beatings at home, still fights with 'outsiders' whenever we went out and, of course, still no money.

In the UK around November 5th each year we'd have Guy Fawkes night in celebration of Fawkes' failed plot to blow up parliament in 1605. It was customary in the 1970's and 80's for children up and down the UK to make effigies of Guy Fawkes from old clothing and masks and stand on street corners shouting "Penny for the Guy" at the passers buy who would, if you were lucky, slip you a few pennies, ostensibly to buy fireworks which you'd set off on the evening of the 5th around a massive bonfire on which you'd burn the Guy you'd made.

Kaz and I would often have no spare clothes to make our Guy with so I'd end up sitting my brother in a baby buggy or a box, stuff his clothing with newspaper to make him look more like a 'real' Guy and put the finishing touches by making a mask from a paper plate and drawing on a face. Pull on a hood so you couldn't see hair or skin and, Bob's your uncle, we had a Guy.

On a good day we'd make several pounds from passers by, which was a lot in those days and, after buying ourselves a few bars of chocolate and the odd comic book, we'd hurry off home and give most of the rest to my mum so that she could either buy dinner or feed the electricity meter.

She never asked, we just did it. Come to think of it, I don't think we ever bought fireworks with that money.

The fighting continued. Both at home and outside.

As kids, we couldn't do much about what went on at home. We were too young, too small and too scared to stand up to my dad, but one evening in 1982 we found a way to deal with the bullies.

After watching Sylvester Stallone in *Rocky 3* and still with 'The Eye Of The Tiger' ringing in our ears, Kaz and I joined our local boxing club and quickly found that we were not only good, we were very good.

A combination of streetwise self confidence, natural aggression and, in reflection, a burning anger at what life had dealt us up to that point made us both extremely dangerous adversaries to face in the ring and we revelled in the attention and praise lavished upon us by the tough east-end coaches who trained us.

Within a very short period of time the discipline and toughness of the boxing training began to pay off. We were both asked to box in competition first representing the club locally, then the borough, then the region and then for all of London. We kept on winning and found our faces plastered over the sports section of the local newspapers almost every other week.

We were celebrities. We thought we'd made it.

We were wrong.

Seems that, whilst your average bully is far less likely to pick on a champion boxer, gangs of kids with nothing better to do but stand on street corners spraying graffiti and smashing streetlamps are less put off from doing so. I found this out when I was 13 or so and was beaten up by a group 16 year olds who felt I was too big for my boots because I'd been in the papers again that week. They decided they'd teach the boxer how to fight for real. And their lesson was a thorough one which included detaching the cartilage from my nasal bone, among other things.

After that, my life became a blur of tit for tat battles with my new 'teachers'. They'd pick a fight and usually win, I'd wait until one of them was alone and get him back and he'd tell his friends and they'd get me all over again. It wasn't great but at least it was predictable. You never had to worry about whether or not trouble would find you on any given day. It would. Always.

You just never knew when.

My grandfather had served in World War 2 with the paratroopers and the S.A.S, or so he'd told me when I was small. I used to love his war stories and tales of secret missions behind enemy lines and was totally army barmy, promising myself that as soon as I was old enough I'd join up, travel the world and live a life totally different to the one I'd been shown up to that point.

I was only 13 so I still had a few years to go but I joined the army cadets to get a feel for what the army might be like. A youth club with combat clothing and rifles arranged around a military rank system, the army cadets became my home away from home for the next few years with almost every weekend given over to assault courses, shooting weekends, bivouacs, survival exercises and adventure training.

I became supremely fit, running 20-30 miles a week with a 35lb pack and gaining my proficiency in numerous weapons as well as gaining the rank of sergeant that required me to learn how to lecture and train the younger cadets in everything from navigation to weapon handling to survival training. I was just 15 by this point and was pretty much a shining star in this closed little community of the cadets.

At home though, it was like we were caught in a time warp.

We still lived in a dump, my dad still drank and hit my mum (though he hit us kids less now as we were getting bigger) and kids in gangs still wanted a piece of me whenever they clapped eyes on me.

I couldn't wait to get into the army.

At 15 I applied to join the 'Junior Leaders'. These are kids who have leadership potential who are to be trained for rapid rank acceleration once they reach age 18. They couldn't, at that time, go to war until they were 17 ½ but they were trained exactly like their adult counterparts . . . though paid much less.

I emotionally blackmailed my mum into letting me join and attended the selection weekend for the elite Parachute Regiment and passed with flying colours. I was still too young to join but they told me that a place would await me as soon as I graduated secondary school at 16 ½. Life was definitely looking rosy.

Or so I thought.

Then, one night not too long before my sixteenth birthday I woke up to the sounds of my mum screaming. My dad was drunk again and showing my mum how much of a man he was. I'd grown up with this all my life and I was kind of used to it and ignored it for a while until suddenly there was a different quality to my mum's screams. A different pitch. One that told me she was in serious trouble.

I jumped out of bed, ran into the living room and headed straight for my dad and punched him as hard as I could in the ribs.

Only I didn't punch him.

As I pulled my hand away I saw that, without understanding how it got there, there was a 7 inch hunting knife that I used on my cadet weekends. It was covered in blood, as was my hand and the side of my dad's shirt from where blood was escaping from the puncture wound to his heart that I'd given him.

I'd stabbed my dad through the heart and didn't even know I'd done it until after the fact.

It was only the first aid I'd been trained in as an army cadet that saved his life and, ultimately, saved me from going to jail for murder. That, and the fact that when he came around eventually he refused to press charges against me.

Soon after I quit school. It was six months until my final exams and I'd done well enough to ensure that I'd pass with very good grades but I couldn't face another day there and instead went off to live in Wales where I could train in the mountains and get fit for the army.

So there I was. Sixteen years of age. Homeless. Broke. Unemployed. Unqualified. Attempted murderer.

Not the typical background for a success author, right?

Yet here I am, years later as journalist, writer, TV presenter, international lecturer, business owner and regarded as a genuine expert authority is not just one but several areas that I work in.

Not only that but I have four lovely children who I'm extremely proud of and a wife that I've been married to for 18 years and love with all my heart.

Yet according to many you speak to it couldn't happen. It shouldn't be possible. Some statistics I've read tell me I was supposed to grow up an uneducated, alcoholic criminal who beat my wife and children and spent up to a third of my life in jail.

Why didn't I?

Well, others still, will tell you that my rocky beginnings created in me a desire to break the mould and fight harder to become successful. It made me tough, or so they tell try to convince you.

I tell you it's neither.

If I or anyone else were merely a product of our environment then everyone brought up in similar circumstances would grow up the same yet they don't.

Some children of alcoholics end up teetotal and some of those from teetotal parents end up with drink problems.

Some people brought up in a life of luxury turn to crime and some of those born to poverty manage to avoid its temptation.

Some children brought up in loving homes become violent to their partners when they grow up and some of those from violent homes are the most loving you partners you could hope for.

Some highly educated children end up on welfare why some who were classified as academic failures become millionaires.

Search all you want but there's no statistic you can find to support the argument that *any* kind of upbringing makes you into the person you've become. There will always be those who defy the statisticians who seem to enjoy pigeon-holing human beings into neat little categories based on geography, race, economics and education.

There's no secret to how they became successful. No hidden formula that you can't learn and apply in your own life. In fact, it's as simple as simple can be.

They made a choice to be different.

They decided that they wanted to act a role in a different story to the one they'd been cast in and they simply chose to play a new part. Nothing more complicated than that.

I did it and so can you.

"You can be anything you want to be in life, just decide..."

"Yes, but if it wasn't for my childhood, my husband, my kids, my job and my lack of money and...."

©Dax Moy 2008

I know it doesn't seem that way sometimes, especially when it feels like life is caving in all around you but nevertheless, it's true. Choose a new role, write your own script, play the part and your life MUST change.

Of course, the only other option is to complain about the role you've been given and yet keep on acting that part. If you're happy with that role then by all means stick with it, if not then get to writing that new script.

Your choice!

Behind The Scenes . . .
The Inspiration For
The MAGIC Hundred

I first came up with the concept of the MAGIC Hundred about 6 years ago after hearing a motivational speaker talk about a man called John Goddard who had become known as *The Real Life Indiana Jones* due to the amazingly adventurous life he had led.

Goddard had lived the most varied and wonderful life you could imagine (I'll tell you more about this shortly) but what struck me most was the fact that pretty much all of what he was able to achieve during his life came about due to what he called his 'life list'.

Now, many stories abound about what led to the creation of this list and, to tell the truth, I'm not 100% sure which one is correct, but the one that I like best goes like this:

When John was a fifteen year old, he got into a little trouble at school, nothing bad, but enough to bring him up for discipline and a good telling off.

The teacher told John words to the effect of "*buck your ideas up m'boy or you'll never amount to anything*" and after some extensive ear-bashing sent the boy on his way.

Later that day when young John arrived home he told his parents of the run-in, and got another round of telling off and the admonishment that *"people who get into trouble or don't pay attention in school end up not amounting to anything or achieving anything in their lives"*

Well, as the speaker told it, young John found being told he may end up a failure twice in one day simply too much too take.

He had to take some action; he had to show everyone that he could be WHATEVER HE WANTED TO BE and that he could do WHATEVER HE WANTED TO DO.

He didn't need anyone's permission to be a success nor would he accept anyone's prophesy of failure either.

John Goddard decided right there and then he would write his own script for how his life would turn out and not accept the limitations of ANYONE who told him otherwise.

(As we'll see later on, this idea of a major definite purpose is a VITAL factor in attaining success in ANY endeavour)

John grabbed a spiral notebook and handful of pencils and locked himself in his room and wrote . . .

. . . and wrote . . .

. . . and wrote . . .

In fact, John spent the rest of the afternoon, into the evening and through until bedtime 'imagineering' the life that he KNEW he would create for himself. By the end of that epic journey into his imagination, John Goddard, a mere 15 year old boy, had created the script for his life and the life of his dreams.

That very afternoon, John had created an amazing list that consisted of 127 totally amazing, inspiring and outrageous goals of every possible description.

Goals like:

EXPLORE:

1. * Nile River
2. * Amazon River
3. * Congo River
4. * Colorado River
5. Yangtze River, China
6. Niger River
7. Orinoco River, Venezuela
8. * Rio Coco, Nicaragua

STUDY PRIMITIVE CULTURES IN:

9. * The Congo
10. * New Guinea
11. * Brazil
12. * Borneo
13. * The Sudan (nearly buried alive in a sandstorm)
14. * Australia
15. * Kenya
16. * The Philippines
17. * Tanganyika (Now Tanzania)
18. * Ethiopia
19. * Nigeria
20. * Alaska

CLIMB:

21. Mt. Everest
22. Mt. Aconcagua, Argentina
23. Mt. McKinley
24. * Mt. Hauscaran, Peru
25. * Mt. Kilimanjaro
26. * Mt. Ararat, Turkey
27. * Mt. Kenya
28. Mt. Cook, New Zealand
29. * Mt. Popocatepetl, Mexico
30. * The Matterhorn
31. * Mt. Rainier

32.   * Mt. Fuji
33.   * Mt. Vesuvius
34.   * Mt. Bromo, Java
35.   * Grand Tetons
36.   * Mt. Baldy, California
37.   Carry out careers in medicine and exploration (studied premed, treats illnesses among primitive tribes)
38.   Visit every country in the world (30 to go)
39.   * Study Navaho and Hopi Indians
40.   * Learn to fly a plane
41.   * Ride horse in Rose Parade

PHOTOGRAPH:
42.   * Iguacu Falls, Brazil
43.   * Victoria Falls, Rhodesia (Chased by a warthog in the process)
44.   * Sutherland Falls, New Zealand
45.   * Yosemite Falls
46.   * Niagara Falls
47.   * Retrace travels of Marco Polo and Alexander the Great

EXPLORE UNDERWATER:
48.   * Coral reefs of Florida
49.   * Great Barrier Reef, Australia (photographed a 300-pound clam)
50.   * Red Sea
51.   * Fiji Islands
52.   * The Bahamas
53.   * Explore Okefenokee Swamp and the Everglades

VISIT:
54.   North and South Poles
55.   * Great Wall of China
56.   * Panama and Suez Canals
57.   * Easter Island
58.   * The Galapagos Islands
59.   * Vatican City (saw the Pope)
60.   * The Taj Mahal
61.   * The Eiffel Tower
62.   * The Blue Grotto

27

63. * The Tower of London
64. * The Leaning Tower of Pisa
65. * The Sacred Well of Chichen-Itza, Mexico
66. * Climb Ayers Rock in Australia
67. Follow River Jordan from Sea of Galilee to Dead Sea

SWIM IN:

68. * Lake Victoria
69. * Lake Superior
70. * Lake Tanganyika
71. * Lake Titicaca, S. America
72. * Lake Nicaragua

ACCOMPLISH:

73. * Become an Eagle Scout
74. * Dive in a submarine
75. * Land on and take of from an aircraft carrier
76. * Fly in a blimp, balloon and glider
77. * Ride an elephant, camel, ostrich and bronco
78. * Skin dive to 40 feet and hold breath two and a half minutes underwater.
79. * Catch a ten-pound lobster and a ten-inch abalone
80. * Play flute and violin
81. * Type 50 words a minute
82. * Make a parachute jump
83. * Learn water and snow skiing
84. * Go on a church mission
85. * Follow the John Muir trail
86. * Study native medicines and bring back useful ones
87. * Bag camera trophies of elephant, lion, rhino, cheetah, cape buffalo and whale
88. * Learn to fence
89. * Learn jujitsu
90. * Teach a college course
91. * Watch a cremation ceremony in Bali
92. * Explore depths of the sea
93. Appear in a Tarzan movie (he now considers this an irrelevant boyhood dream)

28

94. Own a horse, chimpanzee, cheetah, ocelot, and coyote (yet to own a chimp or cheetah)
95. Become a ham radio operator
96. * Build own telescope
97. * Write a book (On Nile trip)
98. * Publish an article in National Geographic Magazine
99. * High jump five feet
100. * Broad jump 15 feet
101. * Run mile in five minutes
102. * Weigh 175 pounds stripped (still does)
103. * Perform 200 sit-ups and 20 pull-ups
104. * Learn French, Spanish and Arabic
105. Study dragon lizards on Komodo Island (Boat broke down within20 miles of island)
106. * Visit birthplace of Grandfather Sorenson in Denmark
107. * Visit birthplace of Grandfather Goddard in England
108. * Ship aboard a freighter as a seaman
109. Read the entire Encyclopedia Britannica (Has read extensiveparts in each volume)
110. * Read the Bible from cover to cover
111. * Read the works of Shakespeare, Plato, Aristotle, Dickens,Thoreau, Rousseau, Conrad, Hemingway, Twain, Burroughs, Talmage,Tolstoi, Longfellow, Keats, Poe, Bacon, Whittier, and Emerson (not every work of each)
112. * Become familiar with the compositions of Bach, Beethoven,Debussy, Ibert, Mendelssohn, Lalo, Liszt, Rimski-Korsakov,Respighi, Rachmaninoff, Paganini, Stravinsky, Toch, Tschaikosvsky, Verdi
113. * Become proficient in the use of a plane, motorcycle, tractor, surfboard, rifle, pistol, canoe, microscope, football, basketball, bow and arrow, lariat and boomerang
114. * Compose music
115. * Play Clair de Lune on the piano
116. * Watch fire-walking ceremony (In Bali and Surinam)
117. * Milk a poisonous snake (bitten by diamondback during photosession)
118. * Light a match with .22 rifle
119. * Visit a movie studio
120. * Climb Cheops' pyramid
121. * Become a member of the Explorer's Club and the Adventure'sClub

122. * Learn to play polo
123. * Travel through the Grand Canyon on foot and by boat
124. * Circumnavigate the globe (four times)
125. Visit the moon ("Someday, if God wills")
126. * Marry and have children (has five children)
127. * Live to see the 21st century

(*Denotes completed goals)

As you can tell, young John was certainly no shirker in the imagination department. He had his goals perfectly thought out and well projected onto the movie theatre of his mind and knew EXACTLY what he wanted from life.

Now, I'm sure at this point you're thinking *"yeah, we've all done those lists but that doesn't mean they come true"* and you know what? You're absolutely right, but you see, this was not just a list to John Goddard. This was an expression of all of John's hopes and dreams, of things, not just that he wanted, but of things that through mental creation he decided that he MUST HAVE!

Again, I'll tell you why that's important a little later but for now, realise that when you move something from the importance level of SHOULD to MUST, things happen in ways that you'd never believe possible.

Back to the story . . .

Over the next forty years John achieved well over 100 of the goals on the list that he wrote back then when he was 15 and stretched himself to achieve challenges that few of us would ever contemplate individually, let alone ALL of them!

But it doesn't stop there!

John Goddard, this real life Indiana Jones, managed to add ANOTHER 400 goals to his list too, making him one of the most richly experienced men on the planet.

And it all began with a list . . . .

Now, when I first heard about John Goddard I was inspired. I mean, here was someone who had gone out and done the very things in life that he promised himself he'd do. He kept his word to himself and didn't sell himself out or sell himself short for an easier life.

Every day for 40 years, this man advanced confidently in the direction of his dreams and endeavoured to live the life he'd imagined and, as Henry David Theroux had promised 'met with success unexpected in common hours'

I think, for a time at least, I wanted to *be* John Goddard and meet with that success myself! Yet, whilst I admired the patience and determination of the man, I was also, at that time at least, a very impatient person.

I didn't want to wait 40 years to list my successes. I wanted them NOW, or at the very least, very soon. I'm sure that as you sit there reading this you feel the same, inspired but daunted at the same time by the patience required to achieve so many great things.

Well, like I said, I wanted my results now, but, how could I make that happen?

After all, it took Goddard a lifetime to get his life list fulfilled; surely the best I could hope for was a little faster? Maybe knock a few years off the time it would take?

But REALLY FAST, well, that was another thing entirely . . . . wasn't it?

I went to bed that night with the thought at the top of my mind 'how can I achieve more, but faster?'

Well, I'd like to tell you I turned all night pondering the problem, but that's not how it happened at all. In fact, I slept like a log.

And when I awoke . . . . well . . . nothing!

No light-bulb over my head, no amazing insight, no divine inspiration.

In fact, I didn't even think of John Goddard and his amazing accomplishments at all.

At least, not until I was in my bathroom, getting washed and ready for work.

About halfway through shaving one side of my face I had a distinct impression of the number '100' flash across my mind as clear as day.

I had no idea how that 100 got there or what it meant but within a few seconds BAM! '100' was there again.

Now, I'd love to tell you that I had some kind of voice or something saying *create the MAGIC Hundred'* but it wasn't that way at all. I simply saw *'100'* and knew, right there and then that I MUST set myself 100 goals and that I MUST be willing to put forth the effort to achieve them all.

That in itself would have been amazing and would have changed my life immeasurably but there was more to my little idea than 'simply' achieving 100 goals.

In much the same way as I just knew that the achievement of 100 goals was to be my quest, I also knew without knowing why, that I would have a timeline of only 100 days to do so.

100 days!

Well, I'd never heard of such a thing.

In fact, up to that point I'd always been told that success and achievement were a 'slow burn' that required patience and careful nurturing to bring about and that to try and 'force' your goals into shorter timescales was downright unrealistic and a sure recipe for seeing your dreams crash and burn.

(Later you'll learn why it's vitally important that you have unrealistic goals if you're serious about success)

Yet somehow, I don't know why, I just KNEW that my idea was going to work.

I grabbed a sheet of paper and began to write down a list of things that I wanted to achieve . . . . and then stopped at about 35.

I honestly got stuck.

I couldn't think of *anything* else to write!

Yet, as I sat there and really opened my mind up to the possibilities I realised that the problem was *not* that I didn't have enough goals.

The problem was that, like most people, I didn't want to give name to many of them because I was scared that I'd never achieve them.

Conversely, I also has a stack of tasks, to-do's and 'chores' that, up to that point, I hadn't even considered to be goals yet, in reality, were just that.

With these two realisations in mind, I decided to write down absolutely everything and anything that I thought would impact positively upon my life no matter how big or small, how realistic or not they appeared to be and, in doing so, opened the floodgates to goal after goal after goal that had been hiding in the back of my mind.

Well, needless to say, my goal card soon filled up and excitedly I read it, re-read it and put it away in my pocket.

With John Goddard's amazing accomplishments serving as the fuel for my own belief and his example of reading and re-reading his list until each of his goals was accomplished, I committed to reading my list as many times as I possibly could over the next 100 days.

I read it when I woke up.

I read it when I went to bed.

I read it when I had a break at work.

I read it while I watched TV, read a book, walked to work . . .

I must've read that crumpled piece of paper 80, 90, 100 times a day and as I did, I noticed a funny thing happening.

Several 'funny' things in fact.

First, I noticed that every single day my list was taking less time to read. It was getting shorter. Goals that were on my list one day simply weren't on it the next because I'd achieved them already.

I also noticed that on an almost daily basis, opportunities seemed to jump 'out of the blue', almost as if the universe were trying to lend a hand to my efforts at becoming more successful.

I wanted money for something, and an opportunity to earn more came out of the blue . . .

I wanted a new place of business; a previously unobtainable venue came onto the market at EXACTLY the price I could afford . . .

I wanted to appear in magazines and on TV and journalists called me to offer me interviews and TV appearances . . . again, out of the blue.

It really was like magic, hence my later calling the program The MAGIC Hundred.

Since I first created the system all those years ago, I have continuously used it to keep me focused and on target and STILL after all this time, things happen out of the blue.

The MAGIC Hundred has taken me all around the world, it has created Luxury cars, luxury travel and an amazing lifestyle for myself and my family along with a six-figure income and an amazingly successful business that generates nearly half a million pounds a year . . .

It has created seminars, workshops, DVD's, TV appearances, writing assignments for some of the world's leading publications and even helped me to create $107,000 in sales of this very book in just the first 7 days of its public release in early 2007.

Now, I'm not telling you this to brag or show off in any way.

Quite the opposite in fact.

Still to this day, the thing that amazes me most about how my life has changed over the last few years and the most 'magical' thing about The MAGIC HUNDRED is this . . .

When I created the system, I had nothing.

I had a part time job that paid me a paltry £5 an hour, a battered and beaten old car, no money in the bank and no obvious means of getting any to pay off the bills and the debts that always seemed to show up when they were least expected . . . or wanted!

No two ways about it, I was broke.

I wanted so much more from my life but had absolutely no idea of HOW I could get my hands on any of the ever elusive 'treasure' that so many others seemed to attract almost at will.

Yet, like many people, I was told to be patient, to bide my time and, most frustratingly of all, to 'be realistic' and that if I did that someday in the future I'd have much, though not all, of what I hoped for.

It was, I reasoned, the sensible thing to do.

After all, it was how most of the people I knew were going through life. Not particularly well off, though not doing too badly either. It was an 'ok' kind of existence where you knew you probably would never get the things you really wanted from life but that you were comfortable enough with where you were to not let yourself be too bothered by it either.

It was the middle ground.

It was . . . average.

But the thing is, I never wanted my life to be average, not for me or my young family.

I wanted good.

I want great.

No, I want extraordinary.

I wanted an extra-ordinary life. One that was so much more than the ordinary that it would seem like a fairytale when it was told and yet, at the same time serve to motivate and inspire others to dare something worthy with their own lives.

I think we all want that don't we? Deep down?

Yet for most of us, when the idea of the extraordinary life occasionally raises its head from its deep slumber, we lack the belief in ourselves to run with it and quickly bury the 'dangerous' thought and return to the relative safety of the average world.

I'd lived that cycle over and over uncountable times myself until that morning when the MAGIC Hundred grabbed hold of me and, in doing so, changed my life forever.

The life I live now is so very different to what it was then and I often have to pinch myself to check that the life I'm living isn't just a dream after all and that it's really happening.

What a change my life has undergone in 6 short years!

And you know what?

Yours could change that way too. It *really* could.

I want you to simply make the decision and commitment to follow me through the rest of this program, inch by inch, step by step and don't deviate, not one bit as I share with you the exact process I and thousands of my readers have used to pour rocket fuel into their goals and speed up their success in practically every area of their lives.

If it helps, think of this program as a map that if followed will lead you to treasure or, if you like, a blueprint that will help you build the life you secretly dream about when you think no-one's watching.

But whatever way you think about it, know this;

The next 100 days of your life are going to pass *anyway* whether you do this or not and, as the saying goes *'time is the greatest currency of all; you should be careful how you spend it'.* If you spend it following the advice I'm giving you then I guarantee you that you'll get more far success than you'd ever believe possible in so short a time.

If you *don't* then you should bear in mind that if you keep on doing what you've always done, then you'll always have what you've always had. If you're happy with what you've always had then great, but if you're not then the only way to get more out of life it to actually DO more.

Luckily for you, that's what this program is all about. So let's get on with starting the process of writing up your MAGIC Hundred goals shall we?

I've divided the MAGIC Hundred into sections to make it easier for you to focus on maintaining a balanced approach to your goal setting.

In the health section we'll be looking at ways to get your and your health into fantastic shape by looking at what's working and what's not in your life and devising a plan for the next 100 days that will change the way you treat your body forever.

In the section relationships we'll be examining the way in which you interact with the important people in your life and devising a strategy that'll have you spending a greater quantity *and* quality of time with them in order to enrich your own life.

In the finances sections you'll be taught the secrets that the wealthy already know about attracting and keeping their wealth that most of those who are struggling aren't even aware of.

In the adventure section we'll focus on putting a little juice and excitement back into your life by opening your eyes to a world of possibilities that you've forgotten about yet which will enrich your live in countless was in no time at all.

In the education section you'll learn why constant learning is vital to your success and how you can give yourself years worth of knowledge in one simple step and guarantee your success in all other areas as a result.

Simply follow me through each section and make sure that you do each action exercise as you come to it if you want to get the most from the programme.

But first . . .

Why You Don't Already Have What You Want

The reasons why you're currently struggling to get from where you are to where you want to be in life are pretty simple and straightforward.

You don't take the time to hear what others are already freely teaching about being happy and successful.

Or you hear but don't really listen.

Or you listen but don't really believe.

Or you believe but you don't act on those beliefs.

Or you act on them but don't really commit to them.

In short, the reason why you don't have what you want is because at every step along the way you chosen to settle for less than you could have. All success begins with choice.

You *choose* to hear what people are telling you. You *choose* to listen. You *choose* to believe. You *choose* to act. You *choose* to commit.

Choose NOT to do any one of these things and you completely change the bearings you've set on your life's compass, meaning that you change the destination you'll arrive at by the end of your life. This destination or, as many call it, *destiny*, is 100% determined by the choices you make throughout your life.

Want a great life then simply start making better choices!

I realise that probably sounds overly simplistic but that doesn't stop it from being true. But it's the *making* of those choices that most people struggle with so let's begin our journey into goal-getting and, ultimately, living the happy lives we dream of where every good goal *should* begin.

At the end!

Anyone who knows me personally will tell you that a favourite saying of mine is that 'you can't hit a target you don't hang' meaning, of course, that if you don't have a clue what being successful and happy looks like then the chances of actually achieving either is slim indeed, if not impossible.

This explains why so many people go through life tired, miserable, stressed out and unhappy. They're seeking happiness but wouldn't have a clue what it looked like if it bit them on the butt!

"Ask and ye shall receive... what do you want?"

"Ummm......"

© Dax May 2008

In failing to decide in *advance* what success should look like *to them* they effectively choose its opposite. Unhappiness.

Let's not choose that. There's enough of that already.

Choose happiness instead.

How?

It's simple . . .

Decide upon the life that you're committed to having and work backward from there. After all, a happy life is simply a number of happy years strung together which are, in turn just a series of happy months and weeks comprised of days, hours, minutes and moments. And every moment, every single moment of every day of your life you're faced with choices about what you want to experience next.

Don't like where you're at right now? Choose an action that will take you somewhere else.

Try This Little Experiment In Choosing . . .

Wherever you are reading this book right now, stand up, move to another room, sit back down and then carry on reading.

I mean it.

Don't just read the words, actually DO THIS and don't turn to the next page until it's done.

DONE IT?

Good!

You can turn the page now.

Well done. You've just changed your life!

It might not seem like much but in very real terms you've just learned the first and most important lessons in achieving both goals and happiness.

Change begins with choice.

Make a choice.

Act on that choice.

Things change.

See, if you chose to listen to what I was sharing with you, chose to believe that my instruction actually held some purpose, chose to act and then committed to following through with that choice then you are now in a different place to where you were just a minute before.

Of course, you may have chosen NOT to get up, NOT to follow my instructions and NOT to change locations. If that's the case then you're in the same place. Nothing has changed at all has it?

That, in essence, is how goal-getting works.

You think, choose, act (or don't act), examine your results, decide if you like them or not then begin the process all over again. So simple, so straightforward yet, at the same time, so unbelievably powerful too.

It means that you can quite literally create your life in whatever manner you choose and it also means that, in very real terms, you can be, do or have practically anything you want simply by choosing.

If that's not been your experience of life up to now and you're thinking this is just a bunch of mumbo-jumbo, metaphysical B.S then please don't switch off just yet. Let me explain it to you.

When I say that you can have anything you want by choosing it, I mean it. You can and you have. In fact, whether you believe it or not, everything you're currently experiencing in life right now is the result of every choice you have or haven't made up to this point in time.

But *choosing* isn't the same as *wanting*.

This is where most people get confused.

Just because you want the house on the hill, the Rolls-Royce Phantom, the private yacht, the close relationship with your partner, your parents or your kids doesn't mean you're going to get it. Wanting simply isn't enough to guarantee the successful achievement of your goals.

But *choosing* is.

Choosing ALWAYS brings you closer to the things you most desire because, unlike wanting, choosing is an active process. Wanting is strictly passive. You'll know when you've truly made a choice to be, do or have more in your life by asking yourself a very simple and straightforward question.

"Did my choice lead to action of some kind?"

If the answer was 'yes' then it was a true choice and you've started the process of bring your goal to life. If the answer was 'no' then you didn't really choose at all. You just wanted. Big difference!

This puts a different light on things doesn't it? It explains why many things you want, even if you want them badly, never seem to come about. It also explains why those people who've already accomplished a great deal have done so. They simply made better choices and more often. They took more action and that action, quite literally, changed their lives.

That's the only real difference between you and them. They kept choosing the same thing over and over until they got it. You either never chose at all or never committed to your choices and instead, kept on changing your mind. See the difference?

There's real magic in this . . . if you choose to use it.

Want more money? Choose it! Want a bigger house? Choose it! Want a better relationship? Choose it!

Want to keep things exactly as they are now? Simply choose it to be so and it will be.

As I said before, change, quite literally, begins with choice.

What do YOU choose?

That's what this book aims to help you to find out. Let's choose to turn the page and get on with it . . .

Why Most Goal-Setting Programs Fail ... And How You Can Avoid Their 'Fatal Flaws'

I wasn't going to write this chapter.

Not because I didn't believe in what I was going to share with you or because I didn't truly believe it could help you to achieve your goals faster. I do and it will.

I was reluctant to write it because when I first thought of it, it seemed like I was somehow being negative or disloyal to all of the great success masters I've read and learned from in the past. It seemed like I was saying that they were all wrong and I was right and that somehow they'd all missed out on something that only I was smart enough to pick up on.

That's how it seemed to me anyway.

So I was going to leave it out altogether. Skip over it. Pretend it didn't matter.

Trouble is, it does!

I don't understand it. I've read EVERYTHING on how to get my goals but the only thing I've gotten is confused!"

You see, whilst the goal achievement and success materials that are already out there in the world are excellent, they require the reader to do many things on faith. To demonstrate belief where belief is already in pretty short supply. Not only that, much of it simply confuses people into inaction by giving people too many principles to remember. A kind of paralysis through analysis, I guess.

That's why I HAD TO add this chapter. In fact, I realised I'd be doing a disservice to you by leaving it out. But just know that whilst my views on the things I'm sharing in this chapter may seem somewhat removed from what you may have read before, that I'm not actually in opposition to the great teachers of the past. The materials they have collectively shared over the years have quite literally changed my life and the lives of thousands of others.

And anyway, now that I come to think about it, I really don't think I'm saying anything that any of them haven't already said, so whilst my way of sharing it with you here may be a little different, my views on these subjects would hardly classify as a groundbreaking revelation to any of them anyway.

So look, as you read through this chapter, don't think of this as an either/or proposition. It's not looking to start a 'my-guru-can-beat-up-your-guru' kind of argument with anyone.

It's not either/or.

It's AND!

Ok, so this chapter is why, despite the wealth of knowledge on goal setting, success and happiness, most people find that the approaches their taught tend to fail and leave them feeling like failures rather than winners.

Let's explore some of the more popular goal achievement beliefs . . .

Do Thoughts REALLY Become Things?

Read just about any book on goal achievement or listen to any motivational speaker for more than a minute or two and I guarantee you'll hear the phrase 'thoughts become things' escape their lips at least once.

The whole 'thoughts become things' . . . thing . . . has been repeated so often that it's now a cliché. But what does it really mean and, more importantly, is it true?

Well, many people will tell you that it translates very literally. Every thought you ever had, are currently having or ever will have is alive and well somewhere in the universe just waiting to interact with something else, take solid form and manifest into our lives as a physical thing.

If you haven't studied metaphysics it's a difficult concept to grasp much less understand or believe but that's what the thoughts become things want you to believe.

Is it true?

Well, given that no-one can either prove or disprove it by any means that scientists agree on being accurate, it's a bit of a moot point. That said, we know from physics that energy is neither created nor destroyed, it merely changes form. From this one perspective alone (assuming that what we know of physics is correct) then a thought is already a thing.

But can that thought energy be manipulated and used to bring what's in your mind to life? That's the *real* question isn't it?

Well, you only need to look around you for your answer!

Every single piece of clothing you're wearing right now, every piece of jewellery, the house you're standing in, the car in your driveway, all of it, every last thing started out as a thought in someone's head yet now as you glance around you it's a real thing in real life.

These thoughts have already become things, right?

But the thoughts become things crowd aren't really using the statement in this way are they? They're saying that any thought held for long enough in your mind must, by law, become that thing in reality.

"Think enough about earning a million dollars and it's yours". That's what they tell us.

And this is where they begin to fail. Not because they're wrong but because they're not telling people the full story. There's more to it than this. If it were as simple as they're telling us then 16 year old boys would be the happiest people on earth.

Just ask your average hot-blooded 16 year old boy what they're thinking about and if they're honest enough to answer they'll tell you that they're thinking of girls. Doesn't mater where they are, what they're doing or who they're with, they've got girls on their mind in some way, shape or form.

"Well, they told me that thoughts become things..."

By the law of thoughts becoming things the likelihood of this young man achieving his goal of manifesting *at least* one girl into his room is pretty high. After all, he's thinking about them all the time, he's certainly desirous of having his goal come to life and his thoughts are so consistent and intense that he should practically be able to materialise a girl in front of him right now.

Yet that doesn't happen does it?

Not for this teenage boy, not for the house you want or the car or the money either.

Here's why.

Thoughts DON'T become things.

Thoughts *CAN* become things.

Confused?

Don't be, it's pretty simple to understand.

It means this; just because you think about a thing, it doesn't mean it will appear in your life. You think thousands of thoughts a day yet you don't see them all magically appear around you do you? In fact, *most* of the things you think about don't show up in your life at all.

But they *could*.

If you took the action required to turn a thought into a thing you could take any thought and bring it to life.

The best way to understand what I'm talking about is this.

Just because you bought all the ingredients for chocolate cake, it doesn't mean you'll be eating cake for dessert tonight does it? There are things you have to do to take the pile of ingredients on your kitchen worktop into a gastronomic feast or they'll simply remain ingredients won't they?

You have to weigh, measure, mix and cook them in just a certain way before they make the transformation from ingredients to the end result of your intention, a delicious chocolate cake don't you?

It doesn't matter how much you *think* of the cake, how positive you are or anything else you may have read about bending the universe to your will, the truth is, as we understand the world right now, if you want to be eating cake after dinner tonight, you have to DO something to those ingredients. Thinking alone just won't cut it.

So too with turning your thoughts into things.

And the good news is that it's a pretty simple process to make the transformation too.

It looks like this:

Thoughts ➔ Feelings ➔ Emotions ➔ Actions ➔ Results (Things)

Let me explain it a little more. This is six-year old simple. In fact, my kids have used this very same process themselves to achieve many of their own goals.

Thoughts when held long enough create feelings of some kind.

Feelings held long enough become emotions.

Emotions when intensified enough drive us to take certain actions.

Actions create reactions or, what we would call results or 'things'.

Nothing too mind-shattering there is there? Hardly rocket science is it? Yet don't let the simplicity of this success 'recipe' fool you. It's the most powerful thing you'll ever learn in your lifetime. It'll bring you *anything* you want!

If you apply this formula your thoughts will quite literally become things. You'll be able to achieve any goal you want. It works every single time without fail and it'll work for you too as long as you apply it.

Here's how.

1. Think about the think you desire as often as you can throughout each and every day. Remind yourself about how serious you are about having it come to life by writing it down on a card or piece of paper, carrying that card with you everywhere you go, reading it as often as you can and talking about the goal to others.

2. Strengthen those thoughts by paying attention to how you feel about the goals. Make yourself positive, optimistic and truly excited by attaining it. Remind

yourself as often as possible that it's not a matter of IF you will achieve your goal or not, but WHEN.

3. Strengthen your feeling about the goal by becoming truly passionate about having it come true in your life. Add as much emotion to the thoughts as you possibly can by listening to uplifting music, dancing, laughing and engaging in other positive experiences whilst thinking about them.

4. Use your passion for achieving the goal to motivate you into taking at least one small action toward it every day without fail.

5. Maintain a commitment to consistent action until the object of your goal is in your life and is now a 'thing' that you can see, hear, touch, taste or smell (of course, I don't recommend tasting your new car . . .)

It doesn't get any simple than that, does it?

Of course, you could just jump straight into the final step of taking action, a lot of people do, but you'd probably find that without the passion and emotion behind it the fuel required to keep you moving toward your goal will dry up and you'll quit before you reach it.

Sound familiar?

It pretty much describes every diet and exercise experience that most people go through year after year, doesn't it?

Let's recap on what we've learned in this section . . .

Thoughts in a truly physical and metaphysical sense are *already* things. Trouble is, it's difficult to manifest those things into our reality without a recipe that involves an element of taking action. You can *try* to manifest your dreams into your reality just by thinking about them but . . . you might be waiting a while.

Does Positive Thinking REALLY Work?

Ever since Norman Vincent Peale first wrote his masterpiece *The Power Of Positive Thinking* it seems that people have gone positive thinking crazy, claiming that it can deliver the results you seek into your faster than practically anything else you could possibly do to achieve your goals.

Is it true?

Well, it's definitely true that a life full of positive thoughts *feels like a better life to the thinker* than choosing the opposite. After all, it's quite a strain going through life believing that everything you're doing is somehow going to go wrong. And yes, feeling better about life is certain to lead to a greater sense of satisfaction and happiness so, yes, there really *is* power in positive thinking.

But does it work for bringing goals to life? That's the question, right?

The positive thinking crowd would like to convince you that it does but, well, I'm not so sure. You see, whilst positive thinking is pretty powerful in the inner world of your mind it has its limitations out here in the physical world.

It's just too slow.

Imagine this . . .

You're out walking on a beautiful sunny day. The sky is blue, there's not a cloud in the sky, the birds are singing and you're feeling great and thinking happy, positive thoughts about life, the universe and everything.

Noticing a busy highway nearby you decide once and for all to prove to the whole world the amazing power of positivity and so you walk out into the busy rush hour traffic, sit down in the fast lane and sit down. With a huge smile on your face and a head full of positive ideas you say "I won't get hit, I won't get hit, I won't get hit . . ."

Ridiculous isn't it?

You just wouldn't do it would you?

Why? Because you know that positive thinking by itself can't change the physical world around you, but rather, it changes how you *feel* about the physical world. Still valuable, still relevant to living a happy life but not the goal-achieving miracle that some make it out to be.

Here's the *real* power contained in positive thinking.

Positive thinking is valuable to the degree that it encourages you to take positive action

Simply put, if you feel confident, happy and positive about something then you are more likely to take the actions required to bring it to life. When you think about it, this is just an extension of the *'thoughts CAN become things'* recipe that we spoke about earlier isn't it? Emotions lead to actions, actions lead to reactions or results, remember?

So here's how to use positive thinking to get what you want . . .

Feel good, happy and positive about the things you want to be, do and have in your life then use it to take action on those things as often as you can (standing up and getting off the highway would be a good start!)

Do You REALLY Become What You Think About?

By now I'm sure you know where this is headed but lets play through it anyway. I'll be quick, I promise.

When you think about it 'you become what you think about' is also just an extension of 'thoughts become things' isn't it? The only difference is that the 'thing' that it addresses is you.

The you become what you think about crowd tell us that the thoughts we think about ourselves become our reality. They're right. They do.

If you believe that you're fat, stupid and ugly, it doesn't matter what anyone else says to persuade you that you're not, that's what you'll see staring back at you from the mirror everyday. Just ask any anorexic how they feel about their 70lb body and they'll tell you that they're fat and need to lose weight.

That's *their* reality and for them it's true.

If you believe that you're smarter than everyone else you know and that you're always right and everyone else is wrong then no-one's going to change your mind for you are they?

So yes, you DO become what you think about . . . in your own mind, that is.

In the physical world where everyone else lives you're not always the smartest person in the room and yes, you're frequently wrong too.

That's the fatal flaw in the idea that you become what you think about. It's more about your internal world than your external one. This isn't a bad thing. It's good to feel good about yourself and believe in our own potential and of course, change always begins on the inside before it becomes reality on the outside but unfortunately most people are unaware of the limitations of this success principle. They think that they merely have to think about who they want to become for long enough and, hey presto! They'll become that person.

Not so.

Try this experiment . . .

Go to your garden and hold the thought that you'd like to grow wings and fly like a bird.

Think positively now, don't forget to smile.

Really intend for this to happen and believe with all your heart that it will.

I'll wait . . .

. . . see any wings yet?

Not even a few feathers?

Thought not!

You could have stayed in that garden a week, month, year or a lifetime and it wouldn't have made a difference. I could have used hypnotherapy to make you believe 100% that you were a bird but you still wouldn't have sprouted wings would you?

So once again a well-meaning success principle shows a slight flaw. Only a slight one, mind you.

You CAN become what you think about if you take the action required to become it. Sure, you can't grow feathers (as far as I know) but you could study aeronautics and eventually create a 'human wing' that would allow you to fly. In fact, someone has done just that already haven't they?

So the truth is, you become what you think about IF you take the action required to become it.

Spotting a theme here?

Time for one more . . .

If You Can Conceive It And Believe It Can You REALLY Achieve It?

Here's the short answer.

Yes.

Pretty much anything you truly believe you can accomplish can be accomplished (Growing feathers is still a problem for most of us though). Trouble is, most people are pretty low in stores of belief.

In fact, they have none.

This is where most success strategies fail. They ask people to simply have faith and believe that everything they desire can and will be theirs if they believe it enough.

And it's true. It will.

But how do you get someone who's low on belief to do a 180 and start believing? It's pretty tough to say the least.

It's like asking a lifelong Christian to convert to Islam or vice versa. It's not like it never happened but it's rare, infrequent and such little demand for it that there isn't a manual for it . . . yet.

'© Dax Moy 2008'

You see, our beliefs are based on our paradigms or ways of seeing the world. These paradigms have been developed over the course of our entire lives by the sum total of ever experience we've ever had. They took a lot of time and a lot of hard life-lessons to develop. They're the compass we guide our lives by and we trust them. To do otherwise would leave us lost.

So, if asking us to change what we believe is not going to work, if we can't suddenly flip a switch and suddenly start believing that we can be, do or have anything we want from life isn't going to work to motivate us into action, does that mean we'll never achieve our goals?

Not at all!

As usual, the answer to this success roadblock is a really simple one yet it'll deliver results out of all proportion to the effort required to bring it to life.

It's this . . .

Suspend Disbelief

You see, whilst we're slow to change our belief systems once we have them in place and whilst we're often resistant to new beliefs that people try to force onto us (even if they're well intentioned and positive), it seems that most of us are absolutely fine with being told to try an idea on for size.

If we're just temporarily testing out an idea we're perfectly happy to give it a shot.

Suspending disbelief costs us absolutely nothing yet opens us up to the possibility of completely new courses of action that we'd never even *consider* taking if asked to suddenly believe.

It's vitally important for you to remember this as you progress through your MAGIC Hundred challenge program. During the next 100 days you'll be as to do a bunch of things that seem a little strange or even downright weird. Just do them. You don't have to believe in them (though you'll get even faster results if you do), but just suspend disbelief and take the actions suggested then make up your mind about whether or not they work for you and if you want to use them again for more results.

Deal?

||||||||||||||||||||||||||||||||||||||||||||||||||||||||||||||||||||||||||||||||||||||||||||||||||||||||

A Personal Note From Dax

||||||||||||||||||||||||||||||||||||||||||||||||||||||||||||||||||||||||||||||||||||||||||||||||||||||||

After beating up on these well known success principles a little in this chapter I feel like I should 'fess up.

I believe deeply in all of them.

I believe that when we become spiritually developed enough we'll eventually be able to manipulate the very 'stuff' of the universe and create the immediate manifestation of anything we desire.

That probably sounds a little 'out there' but I believe it, and anyway, I'm not asking you to do the same am I? Trouble is, I don't know or even know *of* anyone who's accomplished this and neither does anyone else I know.

That being the case, I wanted to share with you a few ways that you could still benefit from these powerful principles in the here and now in a very practical way without suddenly having to believe in a bigger spiritual or metaphysical picture.

So now you know!
∗∗

One More Little Known Goal-Killer You MUST Know About If You're Serious About Becoming Successful

Imagine this . . .

You jump into your car ready to go to work, sit comfortably in the driver's seat, adjust your mirrors, put on your seatbelt and then finally turn the ignition key ready to begin your journey.

The car starts first time.

You knew it would.

It's brand new just out of the workshop, top of the range and has the highest possible grade of fuel in the tank. It's about as perfect as can be and you're excited about driving it this morning.

As you put it into gear and your foot on the gas something strange happens. The engine roars, the car heaves but nothing else happens. No movement.

Puzzled, you give it more gas to see if you can get it to move and you hear the engine roar even louder, feel the car vibrate even more but still, the car doesn't budge.

Frustrated now you floor the gas pedal hoping that this will at last do the trick. It does. The car moves forward, slowly at first then gradually picking up speed but you notice that the revs are through the rood, the engines are screaming and you can smell burning rubber too.

"What's wrong?" you ask yourself.

Then you look down and it all becomes clear. You forgot to take the handbrake off and your foot is still on the footbrake. No wonder you couldn't move!

I'm sure you'd never make this mistake right?

Or would you?
The answer is yes. You would, you are and you have been in every area of your life for quite some time.

Let me explain . . .

When most people set out on a new goal achievement plan of any kind, whether that be to earn more money, lose weight, get fit or anything else they generally tend to look for ways that they can add new 'secrets', strategies and skills that they've learned to their existing lifestyle.

In their excitement to achieve their goals they do exactly as I just described in the previous section and, in essence, put their foot on the gas in an attempt to get to their goal as fast as they possibly can.

Trouble is, most of the time they forget to take the brakes off and end up spending much more energy than they have to in order to get the results they're looking for. In just a short space of time they find that the effort they're expending far outweighs the results they're achieving and, like every other time before, they quit the goal believing that it's just too hard to achieve.

Shame really.

If they'd only taken the brakes off before starting out they'd have found that with just the lightest nudge on the gas they'd have gained momentum and moved forward easily and effortlessly and eventually achieved what they'd set out to accomplish with far less energy and effort than they spent of failing.

That's why during your MAGIC Hundred program you'll be asked at every stage along the way to identify the brakes that will hold you back from your goals. Sure, it'll take a little longer than just writing up your goals lists but the ease with which you'll be able to move forward and gain momentum will be well worth the time you spend doing it.

Very few people know about this success principle let alone talk about it but you do now, so there's no excuse for not using it is there?

Here's How A Famous Abraham Lincoln Quote Can Help You Create The Body Of Your Dreams . . .

. . . And Guarantee That All Of Your Other Goals Come True Too!

It's a funny thing health.

People will pay almost no attention to it until it's gone, and once it has they'll do almost anything and pay almost any price to get it back.

It's true.

Most us go through life taking our health for granted, almost as though it were an infinite resource that will replenish itself without any effort on our part. We run our bodies into the ground, abuse them with poor food choices, toxic substances, lack of activity and lack of sleep and then wonder why the person that stares back at us from the bathroom mirror looks so tired, worn out and out of shape.

Not only do we not look our best but we feel awful too, with the aches and pains of a person much older than we are and energy levels that seem unpredictable at best and at worst are simply not there for anything above or beyond the most basic of the daily activities we engage in.

In short, most of us are sick . . . and we don't even know it!

Well, that's not true. We know it but we call it something else. We call it being 'out of shape' or 'a little overweight' or anything else we can think of to avoid admitting that we've been systematically destroying the very thing that guarantees our ability to get everything else we want in life.

Once our health goes it doesn't matter how educated we are, how much money we have in the bank, how great our relationships have been or how many adventures we've been on, the quality of our life can and will go down. No if's, no but's.

You simply can't live the life you most dream of living if you don't look after yourself.

Just like any other commodity, health and wellness are under the laws of sowing and reaping, requiring that we 'sow' good habits by eating clean, wholesome food and taking part in a regular programme of activity in order that we can 'reap' a well and vital body that will serve us throughout our lives.

You know this already right?

Yet its one thing to 'know' what we're *supposed* to do in order to stay healthy but quite another thing to actually *do* it isn't it?

That's because we forget how important a healthy body is to being both happy and successful in every other area of our life. We disassociate our physical success (or health) from our ability to earn more, learn more, travel more, experience more and connect more with those we love.

Why?

Because we choose to associate pleasure to those things that are harming us whilst associating pain to those things that will bring us greater benefit.

That's why we eat things that we know are harming us and taking us further away from the bodies and the energy we truly want and laugh at the 'health nuts' who eat organically and watch their calorie consumption.

That's why we sit on our butts and watch TV for 5 hours a night and think of those who go to the gym for 3 hours a week as fitness 'fanatics'.

That's why we drink gallons of tea, coffee and soda's and complain about health 'extremists' who want us to add a few glasses water, juice or herb tea to our daily diets.

In fact, most people's beliefs around health are so distorted that they see *any* move toward anything *remotely* healthy as some kind of conspiracy against their freedom to choose for themselves how they will live their lives. Like rebellious teenagers they balk at being told what's healthy and what's not and choose every single option available in their lives to demonstrate their 'freedom' by choosing that which will take them further away from their goals of looking, feeling and performing better than they currently do.

Maybe that even describes you.

Have you found that despite all your talk of making healthier choices that you're consistently doing everything that will lead to the exact opposite?

Most people find that's the case. Again and again and again they make promises to change their health for the better but they never really do.

Until the pain gets too bad . . .

At that point, they look in the mirror and realise that they hate how they look.

At that point they try to play with the kids in the park or walk up a flight of stairs and find that they're exhausted from the effort.

At that point they visit the doctor and are told that their blood pressure is high, their cholesterol is high, their weight is high and that their life expectancy is getting lower by the day.

At that point their life feels pretty grim indeed.

And they wonder how it all got so bad.

Does that sound familiar to you?

If it does then you definitely need to make your health a priority over the next 100 days.

I'm not just talking about going on a diet or taking some exercise.

Sure, those things will be great in the short term but, in all honesty, they probably won't last long enough to give you the benefits you desire. They never have in the past have they?

No, during the MAGIC Hundred programme I want you to go deep. MUCH deeper than you've ever gone before toward ensuring that your health will change for the better and stay that way. Not for a week, a month or a year, but forever!

You see, I completely agree with Abraham Lincoln's famous quote that reads

"You Cannot Help The Poor By Becoming One Yourself"

Most people think that's about money alone but it's not. It's about anything and everything you could possibly ever hope to share with anyone else in your life.

Simply put, it means that you cannot possibly give away to others anything that you don't have an abundant store of for yourself.

If you want to have a loving relationship with someone else but you don't have love for yourself then it won't happen.

If you want your children to grow up happy and healthy yet you haven't achieved that for yourself then you can teach *them* how to do it.

If you want to help others to experience financial success but you can't make your own money work for you, then they're not listening.

If you want those around you to understand the importance of education yet you don't or won't educate yourself then they will never hear the relevance of your words.

If you want to be positive and encouraging to others but your self talk is negative and destructive then your words fall as meaningless platitudes.

You really can't help another gain *anything* that you are experiencing poverty in yourself. It's like trying to lend someone $100 when there's nothing in your pocket, your chequebook has run out, your credit is used up and your overdraft is at its limit. It doesn't matter how much you *want* to help, you can't can you?

It's a physical impossibility.

And that's why health is the 'master goal' that each of us should be striving hardest toward. Because it affects not just us but literally every single person we know, like, trust and love. If our health account is used up then our ability to be the best person we can be for both them and us is diminished massively.

In fact, we do every person, including ourselves, a disservice by not being as healthy as we can possibly be.

I mean it!

If you have gifts you could share with the world but you're too mentally tired to draw them out of your head then you've robbed the world of your contribution.

If your body is so broken down and fatigued through choices that you've made and are continue to make that you can't take a walk around the block with your partner or play with your kids then you've robbed them of the connection and closeness they deserve.

If you're always too drunk, too medicated, too drugged or simply too toxic to function at anything close to your optimal levels then you rob everyone you know of the real you beneath the haze and fog that you're currently living under.

Poor health through disease not chosen by those affected is hard enough to deal with but making yourself too tired, too stressed, too weak, too fat, too broken and in too much pain to live the life you deserve THROUGH CHOICE is just plain crazy!

No one sane would CHOOSE any of those things would they?

And neither should you!

So let's do something about it, yes?

I'm sure that like most people, up to now you've taken your health for granted and not really paid that much attention to it. Be honest, that describes all of us. Even me at times and I'm a health professional.

We're going to change that today.

We're going to set into action a strategy for getting your body and your health back into great shape, removing those aches and pains, shaking out the cobwebs and returning you to a strong, supple, lean and energetic human being again.

It doesn't matter where you are right now in relation to your health, all of this IS possible if you commit to making it happen.

So commit!

Let's start by identifying the 'brakes' in your life that are holding your back from optimal health. You know what they are don't you? Sure you do!

You've always known. You've just pretended you didn't or told yourself it didn't really matter when deep down you knew it did.

That changes today!

In the box below I want you to list EVERYTHING related to your health that you know is not working to create the vibrant, energetic, healthy you that you've always wanted to be.

What's Stopping Me From Being Healthy?		
Dietary Brakes	Activity/Exercise Brakes	Lifestyle Brakes
e.g. I drink too much coffee, eat too much processed food etc	e.g. I sit for too long, never walk etc	e.g. I go to bed too late, don't care for my teeth etc

Ok, so if you actually did what I asked you to do, you should have a list of things related to what you eat, what you don't eat, what you drink, what you don't drink, your exercise, your sleep, your teeth, your hair, your nails . . . . you get the picture!

So what now?

Well, I want you to go back to that list and, in your own words write down WHY these things are keeping you from your health goals.

I know this might seem obvious and you may be tempted to skip this part, but please don't or you'll be missing out on a major part of the process of bringing your health goals to reality.

You see, most of us are so far out of tune with our health that we will tell ourselves lies about the harm we're doing and each time we lie we absolve ourselves of the responsibility for making it right.

Well, I'm not giving you that luxury.

Every time you've failed to achieve your health goals in the past it's because you've told yourself lies.

"Just one won't hurt"

"It's not THAT bad!"

"I'll start Monday"

Now, maybe you don't call them lies but you know they are don't you?

And you know that the only way to counter a lie is to tell the truth right?

So I want you to tell the truth about what your current lifestyle is doing to your health.

Use the worksheets on the following pages to explain WHY these things are keeping you from becoming the healthiest you that you can be then meet me on the page after and we'll continue.

My Dietary Brakes		
Dietary Brake	How Is It Stopping Me?	My New Commitment

My Activity Brakes		
Activity Brake	How Is It Stopping Me?	My New Commitment

My Lifestyle Brakes		
Lifestyle Brake	How Is It Stopping Me?	My New Commitment

Did you do it?

Well done, now we're really getting somewhere!

With your health truths now exposed we can go on to create the plan that will change it all for the better.

I want you to create a list the new behaviours that you will adopt into your life in order to bring about the body, the health and the energy that you really want.

But I don't want vague promises. That won't work at all. It never has in the past has it?

Nope, I want you to list specific things that you are going to do and if you can by specific dates.

For example, 'drink more water' becomes 'drink 2 ½ litres of water every day'

'Exercise more' becomes 'walk 2 miles a day and go to the gym 3 times a week'

'Lose some weight' becomes 'lose 15lbs by October15th'

Can you see the difference here?

We're exchanging the vague, open-ended wish list for specific, goal oriented targets. This gives your reticular activating system something to fix on and something by which to measure its success and in doing so creates a much greater likelihood of it actually happening for you.

That, combined with exposing your own lies and taking away your justification for sabotaging yourself makes this system of health-change extremely powerful.

In fact, if you follow the steps I've outlined in this section and add them to the strategies I'll be explaining a little later on, I GUARANTEE you that you in 100 days you'll have changed your health so much that you'll barely recognise yourself.

You up for the challenge?

How To Build And Strengthen Your Relationships To Add New Depth And Meaning To Your Life

If there's one area that always seems to get neglected in goal achievement programs its relationships. It seems that whilst it's fairly common for people to have goals related to careers, their incomes and their adventures that the very idea of setting goals around their relationships is an alien one.

Shame really.

You see, whilst we often tend to measure our success in terms of the houses we live in, the cars we drive and the money we have in the bank, in reality these are but a small part of success. After all, who wants to own all these things yet have no one in our lives to share them with?

Yet more and more, this seems to be the very position that an increasing number of people are finding them selves in.

Now, at first this may not seem to hold true for you. You may point to your 500 myspace followers, your 357 facebook followers, your 250 twitter followers and any other number of followers.

You may point to the 30 or so work colleagues you speak to everyday, your family, both extended and immediate and, of course your circle of friends and acquaintances-all in all your may number your varying relationships in the thousands (or at least hundreds) and think to yourself if that relationship goals are the least relevant of all the goals you could possibly set.

And you'd be wrong!

You see, whilst the networks of people we now have relationships with in our lives has increased massively over the last few years due to technology and case of contacts, the depth of those relationships has diminished to what could arguably be the lowest point in history.

Just think about it.

The average family doesn't have one single, solitary sit down meal together over the course of a week, with many not over coming close to that number in a *month*!

Most parents don't hug, kiss, or tell their teenage children they love them for months at a time, and many haven't done for *years*! Forget hugging, many parents haven't had physical contact of <u>any kind</u> with their children for the longest time.

And ask any couple you know about what their partners have been doing today and they wouldn't have a clue.

Sure they know where they work and (roughly) what their jobs entail, but fewer and fewer couples know their partners colleagues clients or the people they spend half their time talking to in the various communities they belong to on the internet.

No, make no mistake about this, whilst the quantity of relationships we have in our lives, has increased exponentially over the last decade, the quality of each has suffered as a result.

The truth is, strange as it may sound, people are lonelier then ever before. a study carried out by the Americans sociological review showed that the average person in the U.S has only got 2 people in their lives that they would consider themselves to be 'close' to and the British Journal of clinical nursing report similar findings in the U.K with 1 in 3 people admitting to loneliness in their lives.

And unfortunately, traditional goal-setting programs with their focus on getting up, getting ahead, and getting successful tends to make things worse in this area, not better. We get so caught up in checking off the goal items on our list that we have no time left in our lives for the people we care about most.

Instead of depending our relationships with those people, we make them shallower still by making promises that we either can't or won't keep, and each promise broken becomes a withdrawal from the emotional bank account you share with that person.

You know what that is, right?

An emotional bank account is the amount of trust, caring and affection that 2 people share with each other every time you show the other person that their trust in you is warranted, every time you show them the affection or show them that you care, you make a with drawl.

In this way, good relationships can best be summed up as those who's accounts are in the black whereas relationships that are struggling are simply 'overdrawn' it's a simple way to think about a complex issue to be sure, but true nonetheless.

And now it explains why, when we're operating with a 'full account' we can accept some pretty major transgressions from our colleagues, friends and families whilst at times when the account is low, we 'flare up' at what would seem to be the finest issues related to them.

This is why some people are able to forgive and move on from affairs whilst others still hold a grudge about a forgotten household chore like doing the dishes or bathing the kids.

It's all to do with the bank accounts we keep and maintain with all these we share relationships with.

And its' also the secret to starting, restarting or maintaining a full account with those we most care about in life.

That's why relationship goals are so important to your Magic Hundred Goal Achievement program. During the entire 100 days you'll be topping up bank accounts with the most important people in your life and, in doing so, adding new depth and meaning to each other goals you'll be setting.

If that sounds unlikely right now, don't worry, it always does at first but nevertheless it's true.

Re-establishing and reconnecting with those who are important to you not only helps you to enjoy more of what you already have but also makes the act of achieving your goals that much easier too.

You don't have to believe this right now. But just suspend disbelief like we agreed at the start and take action on your relationships *anyway* and make your mind up at the end of 100 days when you've seen the results for yourself.

Deal?

Right, so we agree that relationship that relationship goals are important to our success and happiness, but how do we go about setting these relationship goals?

Where do we start?

It's simpler than you think.

You can start by making a list of all the relationships you already have in place in your life and looking at them, perhaps for the first time, in terms of what's working, what's not and how you want things to be.

Look at your immediate family relationships first. This could include your partner, parents, children, siblings or anyone else you consider to be your 'inner circle' of important relationships, or those who used to be in the inner circle whom you'd like to attract back there.

Next, identify the kind of relationship you'd like to have with them. BE SPECIFIC not vague. Explain the things you'd like to be able to do together, talk about, experience.

Leave nothing out.

This is important.

The next stage is to identify and remove the brakes.

What's currently stopping you from having the relationships you describe?

What would you need to do to remove those things?

Be truthful about the brakes here.

Don't add obstacles that aren't really there. For example don't say *we're not talking anymore*, when in reality you never 'officially' stopped talking, your communication just fizzled out.

In your ideal scenario, what would happen with regards to this relationship in the next 100 days?

How would you start? What could be some first steps? Identify things that YOU could do to make this happen. *Don't* make your goals dependent on the other person.

Doing something (or not) *"I'll do 'x' if they say sorry"* not just the exercise, just focus on the relationship you want and take whatever steps you feel comfortable with, to bring them about.

Fill in the table on the next page to get a 'big picture' idea of where you stand with your inner circle relationships.

Your Inner Circle

What would be your first step?	What are some steps that you could take to move toward that?	If you did this, how would the relationship look in 100 days time?	What would YOU need to do to remove the brakes?	What's Stopping You From Having This Right Now?	What Kind of Relationship Do You Want To Have?	Name

EXERCISE 2

Repeat the same exercise with your 'middle circle' this could include close friends, extended family and close working colleagues, business partners etc.

Your Middle Circle

Name	What Kind of Relationship Do You Want To Have?	What's Stopping You From Having This Right Now?	What would YOU need to do to remove the brakes?	If you did this, how would the relationship look in 100 days time?	What are some steps that you could take to move toward that?	What would be your first step?

EXERCISE 3

Finally, we come to your outer circle. This could include your distant family, people at work who are not in your immediate area of concern, communities you are apart of, organisations, associations and even friendships you want to develop that you haven't begun yet.

Make that list!

Your Outer Circle

Name	What Kind of Relationship Do You Want To Have?	What's Stopping You From Having This Right Now?	What would YOU need to do to remove the brakes?	If you did this, how would the relationship look in 100 days time?	What are some steps that you could take to move toward that?	What would be your first step?

Congratulations!

You've now got 3 lists of people you already have relationships with and that you'd *like to* develop relationships with over the next 100 days and beyond.

You've also got a fair idea of what the barriers or 'brakes' are around developing them along the lines you'd like to and you also, (As long as you complete the exercise) have the first action steps for developing each laid out for you.

That's the hard work done!

The next bit is pretty simple.

Take Action!

That's right you've got to start implementing the action steps you laid out in the tables above breathing life into the relationship goals you've set.

There is no other way.

You can't sit back and *hope* these things will work out, as you want them to. Relationships aren't developed that way, they require action from you!

But here's the thing . . .

When you start having the relationships you dream of having, the payoff is huge!

Even if you miss some of your financial goals, even if some of your adventure goals fall flat on their face, even if you don't achieve that six pack, or go on that dream vacation by the end of the 100 days (don't worry, you'll achieve tons of this and more if you stick to the program) even if EVERYTHING else was to go wrong for you, the program (and your life) would still feel like a success because you'd have these stronger, deeper, meaningful relationships in place.

And the reason is simple.

The stories of our life's mean nothing if we have no one to share them with, to care about how they turn out and to help shape them page by page, chapter by chapter. It's like that old riddle *'if a tree falls in an empty wood, with no-one around does it make a sound?'*

The answer of course is, who cares?

Same with the stories of our lives; if we own the cars, the houses, the yachts, the jets, the designer clothes and all the cash we could ever want yet have cares or shares in any of it, do we really have wealth or success?

And it'll become more obvious as you start to take action on your relationships.

Now get to it!

Relationship Building Trigger Questions

Stuck for Ideas on how to get started on achieving your relationship goals?

Here are some suggestions to get you thinking about conversations that you could begin having with those people who you want to connect or reconnect with in the next 100 days.

1. **Who have you always wanted to talk to more deeply?**

2. **What have you always wanted to tell them?**

3. **What have you always wanted to ask them?**

4. **What conversations have you left unfinished?**

5. **What do you owe an apology for?**

6. **What does the other person most value in life and why?**

7. **How can you appreciate an opposing point of view?**

8. **What would they enjoy going/seeing/doing?**

The trick here is to dig down and have deeper, more meaningful conversations with each of your relationships and move away from the shallow and meaningless chatter that most of us engage in.

After all, the deeper you dig, the more likely you are to find treasure, right?

How To Finally Gain The One Thing That's Keeping You From Having Everything You Want In Life

Right now, right this instant there's only one thing standing between the life you have and the life you want.

No, its not money.

Money is the RESULT of acquiring the 'thing' you're currently lacking and once you gain this thing you'll be able to acquire increasing amounts of money greater and greater ease.

The thing you lack in order to make achievement of your biggest, wildest most far-fetched dreams come to life is the one thing that most of us seem to dismiss and ignore for practically all of our youth, most of our early adulthood and, for some, our entire lives.

That 'thing' is KNOWLEDGE.

In fact, whoever first said 'knowledge is power' was only partly right. Know ledge is happiness too. After all, the only real difference between you and the people who've already achieved those things that you want to be, do and have is that they know how to get them . . .

And you don't.

Now let's be clear on something before we continue with setting your education goals.

When I speak of knowledge, I don't mean some vague and random acquisition of data or information just for the sake acquiring it. Knowledge is more than reciting the contents of a book parrot fashion in some vain attempt to look smart.

In fact, it's possible to read an entire library of book and never truly gain an ounce of real knowledge at all.

Right now there is more information available to the average man and woman then at any other point in history, yet despite or perhaps because this, the actual number of people who posses any true and genuinely valuable knowledge seems to be dwindling faster than ever.
Everyone seems to have a lot to say about nothing, yet few are saying anything of value.

We now have billions of emails and texts whizzing through cyberspace and the airwaves daily, millions of websites creating billions of pages of content on any subject you care to name and thousands upon thousands of T.V channels and radio stations are transmitting their information to us every second of every day in every country on the planet.

No, we're certainly not lacking in information.

In fact, you could say that right now we're drowning in information whilst, at the same time, thirsting for knowledge.

If you're ever going to be successful, it's time to start drinking . . .

. . . so here's your first sip!

Knowledge is information *applied*.

What does that mean?

It means its information you've acted upon and tried out for yourself so that you *know* whether or not it works for you in your life. That's why it's called <u>KNOW</u>ledge, because you KNOW what the outcome of applying the information will be.

That puts a different spin on things doesn't it?

It means that a lot of things you believe you know about, you don't know at all.

If you smoke yet 'know' it's bad for you, you don't know.

If you overeat yet 'know' that the best way for you to slim down is to reduce your calorie intake, then you don't know.

If you 'know' that you'd be better of starting your own business yet stay on in a job you don't like then you don't know.

The truth is, most of us 'know' very little . . . about anything.

Sure, we have the data, the information and we've read the books but we don't *really* know what these things mean because we've never taken action on what we've learned.
By contrast, look at anyone who is even moderately successful in any area of their lives and you'll be see that they only not gather more information than average person, but they act on it more too.

A lot more!

Again, this is why you have to be very careful about believing well-meaning statements like 'thoughts become things', as you'll end up becoming a thinker instead of a doer. An information gatherer rather than a truly knowledgeable person who has taken action on what they've learned.

In fact, it might even be better if we scrubbed the word *knowledge* from the dictionary and replaced it with the word, 'do-ledge' so that people understood once and for all that they need to DO SOMETHING with the things they learn.

Far less ambiguous, don't you agree?

Why Is Education The Key To Success And Happiness?

As we've already established, the only thing that stands in your way to getting what you desire life is what you currently don't know, either because you don't have the information on how to get it or because you've gathered the information but done nothing with it!

Both problems are easy to rectify.

Ridiculously easy, in fact.

In the first instance, not enough information, the answer is simple indeed;

Get it!

Right now there are more books on any subject you care to name than at any other time in history. On average every one of hose books has taken 10-15 years of life experience or trial and error on the part of the author to put together their version of a strategy that will lead to the successful solution of the problem that their book addresses.

10-15 years!

And you can 'borrow' all those years from them just by reading a book. Of course, you still have to translate their experience into yours, but still, you're getting a lot of someone's knowledge for what equates, in most cases to around a dollar a year.

Would you pay a dollar a year to look over the shoulder of a recognised expert in their field they demonstrated the solution to a problem that you're currently facing?

Thought so!

You see, in very real terms, every single penny you spend on learning the solutions that you, your family, your friends, your colleague or your company now faces is not an expense at all. Regardless of how much you have to spend to learn something, it should *always* be thought of as an investment.

Take that $15 for instance.

Let's say that you take one single, solitary idea from it, put it into practice and it makes you, an extra $30 this year as a result. How would that be? Well, sure, you may think to yourself *"it's only $15"* but if you do you'd be missing the point.

You see, in effect, you've doubled your investment AND gained the knowledge of the author for now and forever. In purely financial term this is a pretty good deal, don't you think?

If you gave me $15 and I gave you back $30 in return you'd be pleased with that, wouldn't you?

I bet you would!

In fact, I bet you'd do everything within your power to *keep on* investing $15 with me as many times as you could, right?

Yet don't forget, you're getting all of my knowledge and experience too which, as long as you act on it, will translate into even greater rewards the more you apply it.

That's why gaining EDUCATION is a vital stop to your ability to achieve your goals and also why a lack of the same will keep you struggling throughout your life.

Revealing The Secret Of 'The Great Formula'

I remember hearing an audio program from that great goal teacher Earl nightingale that explained that there was a formula that one could accurately use to determine the financial success of each and every one of us, and upon reflection I've found it to be amazingly accurate in terms of my own accomplishments over the years.

Nightingale explained that you could accurately judge the potential financial reward of anyone *anywhere* in any job by evaluating 3 things and 3 things only.

How much demand there is for what they do
How well they do it
How difficult it would be to replace them

This explains why a brain surgeon can earn more than a road sweeper who probably works harder everyday who goes home with far, far less in his monthly paycheque.

There are far fewer brain surgeons in the world then road sweepers (demand is higher). We'll assume that the brain surgeon does his work well or he wouldn't be performing surgery, for long and it would be far easier to replace a road sweeper than a fully trained surgeon who spends 9-12 years learning his skill set.

In fact, even if you were the world's very best road sweeper, you'd still fail to command the fees of even a mediocre surgeon because of your replace ability.

It comes back to education in every case.

There will always be high demands for people who know more than others.

People who know more will (unless they have a bad attitude) always be able to do the job better than those who know less.

It's harder to replace someone with detailed, specialised and specific knowledge than it is to replace someone whose knowledge is minimal.

And that's why I always tell people that **success is kept on the top shelf and that the only way to reach it's by standing on the books you've already read**.

Sounds funny, I know, but it's true.

"Well, Dax DID say that success was kept on the top shelf and the only way to reach it is by standing on all the books you've read!'

'© Dax Moy 2008'

I've seen my own income rise enormously over the last few years because of my commitment to expanding my knowledge, and with every book I read, every audio program I listen to and every seminar course I attend I see my income rise further still.

And do will you.

IF . . .

. . . You make a commitment to expand your knowledge base by committing to studying and then applying information that will increase the demand for what you do and how well you do it and make yourself so valuable at what you do that it would be very difficult to replace you.

How do you do that?

Simple!

First, commit to a program of study that has you reading for an hour a day every day.

If this sounds like a lot to you, it's simply because you've gotten out of the habit and instead filled your time with T.V or other non-productive pastimes like, surfing the web, hanging out in forums or updating your myspace profile.

Stop doing that. (Or at least some of it) and instead, claim back 1 hour a day to focus on gaining knowledge. If you committed to an hour a day for a year, you'd notch up the equivalent of around 9 x 40hr weeks across that time.

Don't you think that studying in your field of interest or expertise for 9 weeks a year would make you better at what you do and more difficult to replace than you currently are?

Sure it would, and that's just an hour a day. Imagine if you did 2 or even 3!

You'd soon surpass practically everyone in your field in terms of knowledge, skills and abilities and, in doing so make yourself more valuable to your employers, customers or clients. Which, as we've already seen, will create more opportunity and more money for you to spend on achieving your over goals.

Pretty neat, don't you think?

But where should you begin?

Exactly what should you study?

This is a pretty simple answer to find.

Study the areas that are currently 'brakes' to your already existing skill sets. This means being honest with yourself and asking, *'which areas of my knowledge are keeping me from establishing myself as an expert in my field?'*

For me, as a fitness professional, it was biomechanics. Sure, I understood the basics, but never knew enough to truly grasp why some of my clients were prone to injury after injury despite what I considered to be, great exercise programs that should have made them stronger and less prone to injury, not more so.

Once I was honest with myself about this gap in my knowledge and took action on it, things changed rapidly for the better. My clients stopped getting injured, those with chronic knee, back and shoulder pain healed up, quickly and i soon found myself getting referral from other professionals who were impressed with the results I was able to help my clients attain.
I'm now at the point where students from all over the world travel to attend courses with me to learn, how I do what I do

and my former 'brake' is now an extremely lucrative source of income for me.

That's the power of applying knowledge to an area of weakness.

Take a minute now to identify *your* brakes in terms of your knowledge.

If you're an employee who wants to move up in your company then identify the areas that you think or know are holding you back from that promotion or income increase. If you own (Or want to own) your own company, what knowledge are you lacking that you require in order to get started or make it more profitable?

Be honest.

There's nothing to be gained by pretending you're better than you really are. IDENTIFY EVERY AREA that you know in your heart of heart is putting the brakes on your ability to be successful in this area.

Knowledge Weak Links			
Area Of Weakness	Describe The Weakness	What Knowledge Are You Lacking?	What Could You Do Starting TODAY To Address This?

Now that you know where your weaknesses lie, the 'secret' (Which isn't really a secret at all) to taking the brakes off and gaining a little forward momentum is to take action on them.

Start by reading the books that those who are already achieving the success you aspire to are reading.

Get together a 'BRAKES OFF' reading list and, if possible, order a bunch of them all at once from amazon.com so that you can move fluidly from one book to another as you finish each one. (It takes a lot to get you in the habit of regular study; we don't want the habit to stop because the local bookstore doesn't have your book in stock).

My New Book List	
Subject Area	Books I Need

Next, commit to attending a seminar, workshop or course on your area of weakness at the first available opportunity. It's likely that the thought of going back to 'student' mode will send a few shivers down your spine but remember, this isn't school. There's no real pressure. You're there because you WANT to learn rather than because you have to.

There's a huge difference!

But remember, all the book learning and all the schooling doesn't mean you have more knowledge, does it? It means you have more information.

To turn that information into knowledge requires that you apply real life. This is where most people get stumped. They read the books attend the seminar and came away with a headful of excitement and ideas that they end up with putting by 'for later' (Whenever that is!).

And the longer the gap between learning and later, the less they remember and the less they apply.

Think about it.

In school, every child was taught EXACTLY the same lessons in maths, English and science according to the curriculum of their school. 40 years later, some remember everything they learned whilst others barely remember anything.

The difference? Those that remember actually *applied* what they learnt after leaving school whilst others did so rarely or not at all.

You remember what you do!

That's why my own rule for translating information into knowledge is very simple. For every book I read, I must make AT LEAST 1 new action in my life or my business based upon what I've been taught.

Same with courses and seminars.

Given that I read, on average, 5 books a week this is a lot of new action by anyone's standards, yet in practice I actually tend to take 1 new action PER DAY.

Can you imagine what 365 days per year of applying new ways of doing things would do in YOUR life?

I can tell you from first hand experience, it would change every single facet of your existence. That's not an exaggeration. I mean it.

Again, you don't have to believe that this is true, just suspend disbelief for these 100 days and experience it for yourself to find out the truth of it for yourself, ok?

Now, we've discussed how education is important to getting ahead in your career and finances, but it's also true that knowledge is what holds you back in the other areas of your life too.

What you don't know CAN hurt you!

It can keep you from having the relationships you most want to have, the health, fitness and physique, you most desire and even the travel and adventure you most dream of.

All of these things are currently lacking from your life to the degree that you lack true knowledge about them. Once you gain it, they'll be there sure enough.

So, what do you suspect are the weak lacks in your knowledge in these areas? What things are acting as brakes on your ability to have them in your life exactly as you'd want them to be? What do you need to learn more of, so that the problems you currently face in these areas are solved?

Weak Link Study Areas			
Area	Describe The Weakness	What Knowledge Are You Lacking?	What Could You Do Starting TODAY To Address This?
Relationships			
Adventure			
Career			
Finances			
Contribution			
Other			

Congratulations!

You're just 1 step away from success in each of these areas. That step is to ACT.

What will your very first action be?

Write it Here!

Now go do it . . . TODAY!

How To Generate All The Cash You Could Ever Want Faster Than Ever Before

Money.

It's the reason most of us don't have the things we want in life.

Money.

It's the reason most of us can't do the things we want to do.

Money.

It's the thing that keeps us from being the things we most want to be.

It's true, money or the lack of it is the single biggest reason we can't be, do or have the things we want, and the reason why our lives are in the situations they are currently in.

At least, that's the lie we tell ourselves.

Our other favourite lie is that money is hard to come by.

When combined these 2 great lies create the biggest threats to your success and happiness that you could ever encounter.

They put all your problems *out there* in the land of 'if only'.

"if only I had more money I could live in the home of my dreams . . . ."

"If only I had more money I could take that trip . . . ."

"If only I had more money I could get a better education . . ."

The list of *if only's* surrounding money are endless yet they all come down to the same thing. A scarcity mindset that says *"all the money is* out there *and there's no way that I get any of it, therefore I'm stuck where I am"*

Believe me, I know this thinking firsthand. I've been of both ends of it.

Before I began taking the steps necessary to attract money into my life I used to think it was unfair that those people in the big houses and driving flashy cars had all the money whilst I and my family had to struggles so hard just to put food on the table.

I'd judge them from afar thinking that they must have ripped people off or inherited the money that bought them all of those things they had, for certainly they couldn't have gotten it by honest efforts. After all, I thought to myself, If I can't get these things despite working hard, how could *they*?

I didn't think it was fair that they had so much while I and my family had so little so I was envious and downright jealous of them.

From the other side of the fence now that I'm pretty successful and comfortable financially I find myself one of *them*.

People including friends and family now point all the time that *"its ok for you, you've got the money to do all these things!"* And they're right of course. I do.

Yet none of them ever seem to ask the question *'how did you get from there 5 years ago to here, now?'* Not a single one of them are utilising the same strategies I used for themselves, they focus only on the (apparently) insurmountable gap between the two and take no action whatsoever toward making their financial goals a reality.

It's because, in words of Jack Nicholson in the movie *A Few Good Men*, they can't handle the truth!

In all likelihood, when YOU hear the truth, you won't be able to handle it either.

Few people can.

In fact, when I first discovered this truth about 5 years ago, not only could I not handle it, but I vehemently denied that it could be a truth at all. I was too painful to believe.

So brace yourself.

You Ready?

The truth is . . .

YOU DON'T DESERVE SUCCESS.

If you did it would be yours already!

"What?!!

I thought this was supposed to be a motivational book about achieving success? Now you're telling me I don't deserve it?"

That's exactly what I'm telling you but don't get your panties in a twist, it's not nearly as negative as it may sound.

In fact, it's the very key to your success!

You see, the word *deserve* actually means *'from service'* when translated from It's Latin word roots, literally meaning that the things you have are yours as a direct result of the service you gave up to that point.

You quite literally *'de-serve'* them.

That puts a different spin on things don't you think?

It means that if you're not happy with your paycheque at the end of the month, then it's because your service wasn't great enough to 'de-serve' more.

There no if's or but's about this.

If your service is good enough you can ask for more and you'll always get it. After all, why would your boss say no if you were consistently demonstrating that your service was above and beyond what was expected?

Short answer?

They wouldn't.

Likewise if you own a business of your own. If you're struggling its not because of your location (sure selling pizza in the middle of the Sahara won't help), It's not because of the economy or recession or any other commonly used excuse. It's because of one thing above all else.

You're not giving a good enough service to your customers and clients.

"But we never get any complaints" the struggling business owner cries. You don't need complaints to sink a business. People vote there feet when standards of service are less than they expect and want.

You're either meeting those standards or you're not.

This is great news!
You see, this in itself means that you now have access to the biggest 'secret' for being successful that has ever been discovered.

It can be summarised in 2 words.

GIVE MORE

Whatever you're currently giving isn't enough to get you what you want. If it were you'd already have it and you don't.

So stop arguing.

Give more.

In fact, your mission each and every day for the next hundred days should revolve around the question *"how can I give more?"* and looking for ways to answer it.

Answer this question before we move on.

If I'm your employer and I pay you $30,000 a year for your services and you perform those services exactly to the letter of your contract, never missing a day's work, never arriving late and always finishing your work on deadline, do you deserve a bonus or payrise?

If you answered *'yes'* you'd be wrong.

Why?

Because you were *already* contracted to do those things.

These are the required standards that come with the salary. You've done what's been asked of you and no more, therefore you deserve what was agreed upon . . . and no more.

Note: the fact that many employees are habitually late, take days of and fail to finish there work is irrelevant. Don't fall into the 'well, they do it' mentality. They are not living life to the standards of their dreams either.

On the other hand, if you were to find ways to more your boss's life easier, make your department more productive and make your company more profitable then you've done more than your salary asked for and you de-serve more.

See how it works?

"Yes, but that doesn't mean you actually get it"

If that's been your experience so far it's because you're either not given *enough* service or you've been giving only to get in return.

If the first applies to you then the answer is simple, give more. If it's the second then that answer is simple too. Stop giving just to get. Instead give because it's the right thing to do. Not just for the people you're giving to but for you too.

You see, success isn't so much about the things you *get* for your services, it's about the person you become in the *giving* of them. People know when they're being manipulated and, even if to positive ends, they don't like it.
They feel ill-used and, even though they may still reward eventually, they tend to take longer to do so and reward far less.

On the other hand, gifts of service freely given are always rewarded generously and, in most cases, pretty quickly.

So don't give to get . . . . And you'll get more!

Strange but true.

So, what could you do to give greater service today?

Here some ideas to get you started.

Get in earlier
Stay later
Give up a lunch break to help a colleague
Take a piece of a colleague workload off their shoulders
Send thank you cards to clients
Find ways to cut cost for your company
Automate a process
Write a process map for your job
Organise a staff night out or party
Make coffee
Get lunch
Cover someone's shift
Ask your boss for more work
Get to know a little about each person's job
Suggest ways to improve your customers' experience.
Buy flowers for the office.

Be the 'go to' person on at least one area in your business.
Set up the company blog . . . and post.
Do something . . . just because.

As you can see, some of these ideas are performance based and others are just being a considerate and helpful. All of them, however, are serving *someone*.

Now Brainstorm as many ways as possible to provide a better service to your employers or customers today.

Who Can I Serve Better?	How?

Just this one stop will take you closer to financial success then any other specific action you could take and will pretty soon start paying dividends in your life.

But you want more, right?
Thought so!

How The Wealthy Got That Way . . . Pay Yourself First!

The concept of pay yourself first is practiced by every single financially successful person you've ever heard of and should be practiced by you too if you're serious about getting more from your life.

You see, most people, and particularly those who are struggling financially, handle their money like this;

They pay their bills first (the things they NEED to spend money on), then they pay their 'treats' or the things they WANT to spend money on and then, if they have any left, they put a little aside for a 'rainy day' and pay some money into their savings. In other words, they pay themselves last.

This is the exact opposite of the way that financially successful handle their money.

They pay themselves first in 2 ways that are remarkably simple to employ yet vastly different to the way that most of us earn use our money.

Legal Disclaimer:

I'm not a trained accountant and know nothing about the finer points of the legal implications of any of the recommendations in this chapter as they apply to your specific circumstances. The principles are correct but check out the how you can apply them in your own life by speaking to a qualified accountant.

Use up all of your allowable expenses

Every single one of us, employer, employee and entrepreneur alike is entitled to taxable deductions against certain expenses that we incur in our day to day lives yet few of us are aware of these legitimate expenses, yet alone claim them.

Shame really, because we lose out on hundreds, if not thousands of dollars each and every year by leaving money that we're 100% entitled to on the table and not claiming it.

The wealthy NEVER make this mistake. They claim every single penny they're entitled to and pay only what the law demands of them and not a penny more.

For example, they charge a portion of the cost of running buying cars, their paying fuel bills, running their cell phones, buying PC's, laptops and having internet connection at home against their tax liability for the year (if of course they qualify as legitimate expenses). If their job requires that they wear specific clothing that they wouldn't wear otherwise (including certain types of shoes, suits or other apparel) then they claim that too.

Likewise if they miss meals by working late at the office, subscribe to magazines and periodicals that are related to their work or attend courses, seminars, workshops or conventions that are directly related to their job or their business then they claim the expenses against their tax bills.

All legitimately, all legal and all allowed by the governments of the countries that they live in.

In effect, they get to be, do and have all the things related to becoming a better asset to their businesses without really having to pay for them at all. Their tax bill at the end of each year reflects these expenses and so they pay less.

This is a world away from the way that most people handle their money.

They pay their taxes first THEN spend their money on all of these other things never once realising that they can get that money back through their taxes.

The rich get what they need THEN pay their taxes on the remainder, the poor pay their taxes first THEN try to get what they need from what's left.

Big difference!

So what can you do about it?

Well, like I said earlier, I'm not an accountant and, chances are I don't even live in your country so it would be wrong (and illegal) to offer you financial advice, but the first step you should take is to go consult an accountant about where you could start reclaiming expenses that you're currently spending out on yet not recovering from your tax bill.

Most accountants offer a free initial consultation so there's no real expense to you but here's the thing. Even if you have to pay, the accountant is a legitimate expense against your taxes anyway so, essentially, they're free anyway!

The money they'll save you will ALWAYS be far, far more than you'll ever spend on them so act now, don't delay. You're bleeding money away and you don't even know it!

But That's Not The Only Way That The Wealthy Pay Themselves First . . .

They also pay themselves first . . . literally.

They put aside 10% of their income BEFORE they pay their bills THEN pay for their needs and their wants with the remainder.

Do you grasp the implication of this?

Their success is assured because they never leave their savings to chance or decide whether or not they can afford to save this week or this month. They pay themselves first then everyone else after!

When I first came across this concept I played with the idea a bit but thought it was a bit much to ask me to do in reality. Particularly as, at that time, I was living pretty much from paycheque to paycheque with literally nothing to spare. Or so I thought.

Yet I decided I'd give it a go. If it was too difficult I could easily change things I thought.

Now, I'd love to tell you that putting aside the first 10% of my meagre pay was easy, but I'd be lying, it wasn't.

In fact, I found it tough for the first few months, but somehow, the bills still seemed to be getting paid and we still had food on the table so I continued the practice.

Pretty soon, there was a month's pay sitting in my account, then two, then three and, better still, it was earning me interest. Ok, not a lot at first but I'd never even had savings before then so this was a big deal.

In fact, it was this very practice of paying myself first that paid for my first studio, then my second then my third and it continues to bring me opportunities for expansion and growth to this day.

It'll do the same for you too if you allow it.

Simply start today to pay yourself 10% of everything you earn, no matter how big or how small. Just do it.

Open a 'paying yourself' bank account that is untouchable. You don't use it for holidays or clothes, but for generating interest and for allowing you to take up the opportunities that come your way in life.

Ok, so now you're got a system for giving better service and for keeping more of what you earn. This puts you in a better position for becoming financially successful then fully 80% of every person you'll ever meet.

Well done!

Your financial mindset is really shifting already!

But you *still* want more don't you?

Well how about this?

I call it . . .

The Gun To The Head Financial Success Strategy That Will Save Your Life

Yes, I know it's not customary for success books to use negative imagery but there's no getting around the fact that its an image that seems to work for practically everyone who uses it and I know it'll work for you too . . . if you apply it.

It's a simple enough strategy really.

Very simple in fact.

It asks you to imagine that your life literally depended upon you finding a way to reach your financial targets. Lets for arguments sake say it's $100,000.

127

Imagine that someone held a gun to your head and threatened to pull the trigger if you didn't find a way to come up with ten grand in the next 100 days. Imagine also that they stipulated that you couldn't get it by illegal or dishonest means and that you weren't allowed to borrow it.

The money would have to be yours free and clear or BANG! Game over.

What would you do?.

Now apart from the obvious answer of I'd be terrified and beg for my life (they can't be reasoned with) or "try to fight and disarm them (there a fully trained special forces operative) you should have come up with a third answer that involved someone getting the cash.

But how would you do it?

Would you look for the big $10,000 payoff in one hit?

If so, what could you do that would generate $10,000 quickly?

Would you 'chunk it' into smaller amounts?

You could look for multiple ways to earn 2x $5,000 or 3x$3333 or even 10 x $1000, couldn't you?

Or would you break it down into a TDE or target daily earnings goals that enabled you to track your progress towards the goal every day of the 100 days?

In this instance you know that you'd need to achieve a TDE of $100 a day more than you currently earn to make your $10,000.

There isn't a wrong answer here.

They are ALL legitimate ways to hit the target yet most of us don't even consider how they may be attained, instead we focus on how big the goals is and how far away we are from achieving it.

We get intimidated by the problems rather than inspired by how achievable it really is if we apply solution-based thinking to it.

Not you though, right?

You're going to put the plan in place to make your financial goals a reality by looking at them through solution-tinted spectacles that open you up to the possibilities before you rather than showing you why they're ridiculously unrealistic aren't you?

So lets look at each method of making the $10,000 and see how we could do it shall we?

The first thing I want you to do is approach these exercises with 'blue sky' thinking, meaning that you don't censor yourself in any way, shape or form. Don't look for reasons why you wouldn't be able to do these things or focus overly much on how you'd do them, just focus on what you'd do and nothing else.

Now, grab a stopwatch or timer and set it for 2 minutes. That's how long this exercise is going to last.

You have 2 minutes to think of as many ways as possible to make $10,000 in a single big payday. Keep your pen moving for the entire time, don't stop, pause or over think things, just search for answers.

Ready?

Go!

How Could I Earn $10,000 In One Big Hit?	

Well how did you do?

Chances are that initially you were a little stuck for ideas yet once the first few trickled out the rest came easier and easier, right?

You probably found too that the ideas were things that you've thought of and yet dismissed in the past as 'silly' or unrealistic yet now with that gun at your head they're not so silly are they?

Funny how the brain works when you demand a solution of it isn't it?

Let's try it again, this time with chunking

This is normally much easier as you can break the goal into smaller parts that you may have already accomplished or came close to in the past.

130

Just focus on breaking that $10,000 into as many large to medium 'chunks' as you can think of in 2 minutes and keep that pen moving.

Ready?

Go!

How Could I Earn $10,000 In Chunks?	

How did you do this time? Easier right?

You probably thought of 20 or more ways to earn between $1000 and $5000 pounds didn't you? In fact if you were to total up the potential revenue form that exercise you'd probably find you at least doubled the $10,000 target I set for you because the numbers are smaller and less intimidating.

This is just another example of why taking a big goal and breaking it into chunks can be a very effective goal achievement strategy, as you tend to see more opportunities for their achievement.

Ok, now for the final exercise in this section.

This one is simplest of all. You have to earn an extra $100 a day for the full 100 days.

Just a $100. You could do that couldn't you?

Lets see shall we?

2 minutes!

How Could I Earn $100 a Day For 100 Days?	

How did you do?

Easiest of all, right?

$100 can be made quite easily by taking on an evening job, doing overtime, or any number of other things that many people know but haven't really considered taking action on.

The gun to the head makes you consider them, right?

Now, don't worry if you got stuck on these exercises, many people do first time out. They're just not used to blue sky thinking.

That's why you need to practice this daily as part of your power questions. When you start looking for possibilities as part of your daily strategy, a funny thing happens . . . you find them.

Now here's an example of the same 3 exercise that I did as part of writing this chapter.

Note: I'm sitting at the kitchen table at home with my ipod timer running so I'm only taking 2 minutes too!

How Could I Earn $10,000 In One Big Hit?	
Create a new weekend course for trainers	
Run a success seminar	
Create a high-end personal training camp	
promote my new mentor program	
Put on a 2 day sale of Magic Hundred	
Write and record a new goal achievement program	
Write a marketing program for trainers	
Create an international association	
Write a new book	
Record an audio program	

How Could I Earn $10,000 In Chunks?	
Seminars for coaches	
Seminar for public	
Teleseminar for trainers	
Teleseminar for public	
Sixpack abs program	
Nutritional coaching program	
Run a challenge makeover competition	
Write a 6 week program E-book	
Create a membership site	
Affiliate sales	
Co-create products	
Create a fitness vacation	
Create a overseas retreat	
Create a marketing bootcamp	
Design and promote a course	

How Could I Earn $100 a Day For 100 Days?	
Affiliate	
Sell3 E-books	
Look online for other prouducts	
Create $10 product and sell 10	
Increase fees at studios	
Do 1 extra appt per day	
Create low-cost seminar	
Weight management course	
Goal mastermind	
Create Recurring revenue product	
Clickbank	
Sell 1 excellence module a day	

The amazing thing is that I've just uncovered not $10,000 but hundreds of thousands of dollars and the ideas were there all along, right there in my head!

I didn't need to learn anything new, spend any money or receive training of any kind to uncover them, and neither do you.

And the best thing of all is that the only thing standing between where you are right now and actually making any one of these money generators come to life is the decision and commitment to act upon them.

Just think what you could achieve!

And you're not limited to $10,000 either. Your goals can be as big as you like and all you have to do is go through the same processes that has been laid out over the last few pages.

For example, if I wanted to earn $1000,000 over the next 100 days, I'd need to earn $10,000 a day. Knowing this I can turn my mind to that goal and open up a series of $10,000 a day solutionS.

Exciting isn't it?

But it's not enough to just set random financial goals and hope to achieve them. Money rarely, if ever serves as a good motivator in and of itself.

It's the things that money allows us to be, do and have that make the pursuit of money a worthwhile endeavour, not the acquiring of the money itself.

In fact you could say that money itself has no value of its own, regardless of what's printed on the notes in your wallet. It's just paper it only becomes of value at the point where you use it in exchange for the things you want to experience in your life.

This is why whenever you set a financial goal for yourself, you should always attach meaning for it by describing what this sum would allow you to be, do and have once you acquire it.

As well as adding more meaning to becoming financially successful, this allows you to maintain higher levels of excitement, passion and purpose around them meaning that you're for more likely to keep taking the actions required to bring them to life.

So one last time, let's look at this section again.

1. Choose your financial goals be specific write down the exact amount you want to earn in the next 100 days

2. Attach a specific be-do—have value to the financial goals you've set

3. Break it down with 'blue-sky' thinking by giving yourself 2 minutes to think of as many ways as possible to earn that amount in a single lump, in 'chunks' and in 100 bite size pieces spread evenly across the 100 days.

4. Finally, write down the first steps you're going to take to bring your financial goals to life which projects will you commit to and how will you start?

5. Bring the whole thing together by stating your financial goal in the following manner . . .

I am so happy and grateful to have accomplished my financial goal of acquiring (amount) in 100 days beginning (date) and ending (date). My chosen strategies for accomplishing this ARE (name your stategies) and have allowed me to BE-DO-HAVE the following things) in my life.

Now get to it!

Here's How To Plug Your Life Back Into The Mains . . . And Crank Up The Juice!

Adventure.

The dictionary says that the word means 'an unusual and exciting experience'.

In many respects, I guess you could say, it's what life is supposed to be about; Adding new and rewarding things that stretch our limitations and give new meaning and direction to our lives.

Yet sadly, for most of us, our lives are anything but adventurous.

In fact, most people's lives are repetitive and boring!

Day in, day out we gravitate toward the same activities, same thoughts and same feelings . . .

. . . and wonder why our lives aren't getting any better for us!

Remember that definition of madness I described earlier? The one about doing the same things and expecting different results? If this doesn't fit that description, I don't know what does!

Yet it's so easy for us not to fall into this trap. All we have to do is focus on adding new, unusual or exciting experiences to our lives.

That's 'ALL'.

So why don't we?

To be honest, it's because most of us don't really know where to start when it comes to making our lives more exciting. We're so caught in a rut that rather than exciting, everything seems 'dangerous' and fraught with risks that we feel compelled to avoid so that we can stay where things are 'safe'.

The only trouble is, that safety is an illusion. It's a trap.

Safety, for most of us simply becomes 'what we know' and what we're comfortable with which means that new, unusual or exciting just never happens . . . . and we're back to square one!

But what can we do about it?

Well, the first step is really quite simple. We need to define what 'adventure' means to each of us individually and create a mental 'recipe' for what an adventurous life would involve.

For example; I'm a former soldier so my definition of adventure incorporates a love of climbing, kayaking, parachuting and roping out of helicopters and such. I find this really exciting and define adventure as things include an element of physical danger along with travel to exotic locations like deserts, jungles and mountains. This is my recipe for adventure and really motivates and inspires me.

I feel happy and hopeful to the degree that I have these things in my life and less so when they are absent on not on the horizon any time soon. I guess you could say it's what gives my life 'juice'.

To put it another way, you could say that they make me more . . . me!

I have come to identify myself as a person who travels a lot, takes regular off-the-beaten-track adventures and, quite often engages in activities that many people would consider to be too dangerous or high-risk. It's not that I don't see their point. I do. Some of them really are quite risky, but nonetheless, they help me become more of the person I wish to be and so, for me at least, the benefits outweigh the risks by a fair margin.

In fact, I believe the biggest risk we truly take in life is to play it safe by never taking risks, never stretching ourselves and never experiencing the things that, in our heart of hearts, we always really wanted to experience.

> We all have places we want to see before we die, don't we?

> We all have things we'd like to do.

> We all have skills we'd like to learn.

> We all have languages we'd like to speak.

> We all have musical instruments we'd like to learn to play.

ALL of this is part of this great adventure we call life. Quite literally, any of these things can classify as exciting and unusual if YOU say they are. If the thought of experiencing them excites you and involves doing things that are out of the ordinary as you define your life, then you're experiencing an adventure.

If, on the other hand, you're living your own version of the Bill Murray movie *'Groundhog Day'* and finding that your life is full of repetitive experiences that you find boring, dull and lacking in excitement then you really need to get some adventure into your life, and quick.

This isn't just desirable, it's essential!

You see, life is really about nothing more than writing out our own stories about what things mean to us and we're happy to the degree that our stories and our lives have meaning. By contrast, we become less and less happy when what we're experiencing has no obvious meaning attached to it.

So the question is, what story to you want to write on the pages of your life-book?

Do you want *"Got up, got the kids ready for school, did the dishes, watched TV, tidied the house, collected the kids, cooked dinner, had a bath, watched TV, went to bed"* on every page or do you want your pages to read *"Watched the sunrise from a tropical beach, played the guitar sitting on the front porch with my kids, climbed a mountain to see the sunset, learned to tango . . ."* and any number of other things.

Neither is more right than the other, rather it's what's right for you. What would make YOU happiest?

I know that for me the last few years have been an amazing journey into writing the chapters of my own life-book.

In just 4 years I've:

Travelled all over Thailand over 18 separate visits, including mountains, cities, jungles and tropical islands

Visited the ancient temple ruins of Angkor Wat in Cambodia

Travelled practically the full length of Vietnam

Completed 2 separate 1-month 'outback' adventures in Australia including Kakadu National Park, The Daintree Rainforest, The Great Barrier Reef, The Blue Mountains and Ayers Rock

Stayed in luxury hotels in Nice, Venice Monte Carlo and Lake Como and campsites in Britain, Tuscany and Australia

Visited the Coliseum in Rome, the Leaning Tower in Pisa, the Pyramids in Egypt, Ice hotels and the Northern Lights in Norway and yes, even Disneyworld and Universal studios in Florida (twice)

I've run ultradistance marathons in the Amazon Jungle, freefall parachuted over the Great Barrier Reef with my then 15 year old daughter Kayleigh, swam in rivers with Pirhana, and in lakes with crocodiles, SCUBA dived with manta rays and been attacked by deadly snakes on forest trails.

I've even lived through a Tsunami with my family (we were actually IN the water!).

All in all, you could say I've had a pretty adventurous few years and, the best bit for me is that I know that there's more to come, more to see, more to do and experience so that I can add some pretty great pages to my already interesting life-book.

For me this has all added an amazing richness and excitement to my own life and given me even greater power, passion and purpose toward helping other people experience more in their own lives.

But what about you?

Would you find all this an exciting and inspiring adventure or a waking nightmare?

Does the thought living the adventures I described above excite you or repel you?

There's no right or wrong here, so don't feel that your adventure goals in any way have to mirror mine. They don't. As I've already explained, your definition of adventure is for you to decide.

It might be to climb Mount Kilimanjaro, Freefall parachute jump over the great barrier reef, travel to Tibet, learn to ski, drive a race-car, cycle across Vietnam, appear in a play, write a book, play the violin, speak fluent Thai, change jobs or move home or know and experience every position in the Kuma Satra.

It could be literally ANYTHING you want it to be . . . as long as it excites you AND stretches you, even if only a little bit, to take action outside of your comfort zone, or at least the edge of it on a regular basis.

Just like when you were a kid.

Back then, every single day of your life was an adventure. You'd think brand-new thoughts and do new and scary things and bit by bit you stretched yourself and your boundaries to become who you are today.

Yet somewhere along the way that daily adventure stopped.

Either because you were told that it was time to 'grow up' (whatever that means) or because you felt, or were made to feel that your dreams of adventure were silly and juvenile in some way.

They were not. They were (and are) the very stuff that your life is made of and to deny them is to deny your true self of the opportunity for real joy and happiness.

I know this to be true every time I watch my eight year old son Connor playing or talk to him about the life he's Imagineering for himself.

It's FULL of adventure!

He's not talking of money or houses or owning things or saying 'I just want to be secure, Dad'. He's talking about things that he's going to DO, places he's going to GO, or what he's going to BE. And the difference between Connor (or any five-year old for that matter) and most adults is that he actually believes what he's saying and because he does, he's happy nearly all of the time.

Learn from an eight year old.

Bring back some real adventure to your life.

Take the time now to create a list of things that you'd REALLY like to do or places that you'd really like to go to in the next 100 days.

Really stretch your mind and let your imagination run wild and write down as many adventure ideas as you can.

Don't limit yourself by telling yourself you won't or can't do something, just create your list.

I know it seems unlikely but I guarantee you that once you create your list you'll start to experience more adventure straight away. In fact, creating the list is a kind of adventure in itself right?

I mean, if you're writing down things that you truly want for yourself over the next 100 days then you've got to be excited right?

Well THAT'S an adventure isn't it?

Write your list now and generate as much adventure as you can stand in your life for the next 100 days. Get out of your comfort zone and challenge yourself to add new, unusual and exciting experiences to your life.
Use a 'blue-sky' approach on the list below. Pretend money isn't a issue and just write down what you WANT to experience in this area.

Adventure Brainstorm List		
What Places Do You Want To See?	What Things Do You Want To Experience?	What Would You Like To Learn?

Creating Your MAGIC Hundred Action Plan

If you've been following all of the steps I've laid out throughout this book and you've been writing your down your goals that relate to your health, your relationships, your finances, your education and your adventures, you should have a pretty extensive list of things that you want to do with your life over the next 100 days.

Perhaps this is the first time you've thought of any of these things . . . in a serious way, at least.

At this stage you're probably a little daunted at the size of the undertaking and, if you're like most people, already convincing yourself of the impossibility of the task ahead of you.

Don't!

Remember, you don't even need to believe in your ability to achieve these things right now. Just make sure you suspend disbelief, carry out the steps described in the previous sections to the best of your ability and enjoy yourself. This is, after all, your MAGIC Hundred program isn't it?

YOU chose the goals; they weren't forced on you, so just have fun with it. It's just a game. You can always play it again, right?

You definitely don't want your brain to carry out the command *'this is impossible'* do you?

So whenever you're bombarded by a negative *'I can't do this'* thought, remember that **thoughts CAN become things** and rapidly convert your thoughts into *'I WILL do this'* and immediately put your mind to an action that you can take toward achieving one of your goals.

This is really powerful and will ALWAYS get you through those negative periods that you will undoubtedly face over the next 100 days.

Positive action the only reliable way there is to counter negative thought so use it and use it often over the next 100 days and you'll do just fine.

Ok, let's back to those lists of yours shall we?

At the moment they're a jumbled mess, a mish-mash of probably hundreds of things that you want to be, do and have in your life. The trouble is, that as things stand at the moment, your goals are in chaos, and that's contributing to the uncertainty that you might be feeling at the moment.

Don't worry. We're going to make them a lot more ordered and a lot more structured for you so that you start to get a real sense that your goals can and will be achieved.

But where do we start?

Well first of all, you've probably found that you've created a list that adds up to much, much more than a hundred goals so we're going to start by chopping that down into a more manageable size and focus on the goals that most inspire us.

To do this, you'll need to take every single goal that you've created on each of the tables throughout the program and add it to the goal grade table below.

Yes, it'll take a little while to collate them all but it's well worth it.

Do it now.

MAGIC Hundred Goal Grader			
Goal	Grade	Goal	Grade

MAGIC Hundred Goal Grader			
Goal 51-75	Grade	Goal 76-100	Grade

MAGIC Hundred Goal Grader			
Goal 101-125	Grade	Goal 126-150	Grade

MAGIC Hundred Goal Grader			
Goal 101-125	Grade	Goal 126-150	Grade

What you've just completed is your first draft at your master list. Now it's time to find out just how important they really are to you!

Simply work through every goal you've written up and grade them A, B or C.

A goals are those that you feel REALLY motivated to achieve and really dedicated to having come true for you in the next 100 days. I don't want you to worry about whether or not they're *possible* at this stage, just make sure that you feel energy coming from them ok?

B goals are those that you feel strongly connected to, you'd really like for these things to happen but, well, they don't call out to you in the same way as your A goals.

C goals are those goals that you feel would be 'nice' to do or 'nice' to have and that you'd like to achieve 'someday'. In short, they don't call you in the same way as you're A's and B's.

Again, this grading is totally down to you. If finishing tiling the bathroom is more important to creating the life of your dreams than climbing a mountain, that's fine, just make sure that you 'own' your answers ok?

Right, go off and do that now before you turn the page.

Done that?

Good!

Now, take you're A and B goals and insert them into the 'MAGIC Hundred Master List' below.

MAGIC Hundred Master List		
Goal	Who Can Help?	What Is The First Action I Can Take?

MAGIC Hundred Master List		
Goal	Who Can Help?	What Is The First Action I Can Take?

MAGIC Hundred Master List		
Goal	Who Can Help?	What is The First Action I Can Take?

(If you still have more than a hundred, then you might need to repeat the process with your remaining goals. If you have less, then simply add some of your C's into the list or think of some better ones.)

On the master list you'll notice the columns that say "What is the first thing you could do toward this?" and "Who could help you with this?"

We're going to tackle these next.

Looking at the first column "what is the first thing you could do toward this?" I want you to think of the very first teeny-tiny stepping stone that will start the journey.

For instance, if one of your goals is to take an expensive, luxury holiday that is currently outside of your comfort zone as far as cost is concerned, the first step could be . . . *get a brochure,* for example.

Now, I know that browsing a brochure doesn't mean you'll go, we've all looked at brochures before, but it's a start. It's action. It's a step. And as the famous Lao Tsu quote tells us *'The journey of a thousand miles begins with a single step.'*

The next steps might be to sit down with a travel agent, then send for an online quote, then compare prices, then speak to boss about potential of overtime or a raise, then start saving £30 a week.

You can follow this process for all of your goals, but regardless of the action, the most important thing is to take that first step.

So, what are the first steps you could take with *your* MAGIC Hundred?

Go write down your first steps now then come back when you're done.

The next part of the process is to fill in the box that says 'who could help you with this?'

It's strange, but the feeling that we have to do everything ourselves is so pervasive in society that we have developed into isolationists, each carrying the weight of our own respective worlds on our sagging shoulders.

The sad thing is that most of us have within our sphere of contact, enough knowledge, skills and ability at our disposal to actually achieve almost anything we want.

The trouble is, we don't ask!

It's true you know, for most people, the only thing stopping them from achieving the success they desire in life is the failure to ask for help.

Instead they say to themselves *'nope, I'll either do it alone or I'll not do it!'*

Basically, they condemn themselves to failure!

Yet even the most rudimentary study into the lives of successful men and women will show you that success is only achieved through interdependence and co-operation with others.

Indeed, Napoleon Hill, the famed author of *Think and Grow Rich* said that when two minds get together, they create a third mind more powerful than the sum of both combined. He called this the mastermind principle and its power has been proven again and again.

I myself am involved in several mastermind groups and can attest to the power and energy that they produce toward achieving great things. In fact, many of my successes I attribute directly to my participation with my masterminds.

That's why we're going to use the mastermind principle within the MAGIC Hundred by asking upfront, *'who can help me?'*

Go through the list and answer that question for each of your goals.

Maybe it'll be a your spouse or your kids, maybe a work colleague, maybe a lifecoach, a personal trainer, a local business person, an old school teacher, a celebrity.

Just write down your answer to the question who can help me and see who first comes to mind.

(a word of advice, don't ask people who are negatively minded or who you know in advance will say no. Ask only positive people)

If no-one just yet, that's fine, just move onto the next goal and write your answer. You can always come back and redo the ones you miss.

Once you have your list of what I call success conspirators, you need to actually ask them for help!

This is where most people get stuck. They think to themselves *'I can't just go ahead and ask!'* and, well, they don't.

End result? They get no help and their goal grinds to a halt.

I don't want this to happen to you. I want you to take that step of explaining to your success conspirators exactly what you're trying to do in the next 100 days and ask them what they think would be the best way to go about achieving your goals.

When they answer you, ask them simply, politely and directly if THEY will help you.

Ok, some people might say no, but I think you'll be surprised at just how many people will be happy to lend a hand to someone with a goal who is determined to take action on it.

The basic rule is ask.

Ask early, ask late, ask once, ask twice, ask anyway you please, but ask.

You get the message!

How To Stay On Track, Keep Going And Make Sure Life Doesn't Get In The Way

Before I start this section, I'd just like to say congratulations.

You know, it's been quoted that over 80% of people who start a book or buy an audio programme never even reach the second chapter, and here we are in the final straights of the MAGIC Hundred and you're still with me.

That's excellent!

That means that you're the sort of person who's committed to seeing things through to the end. In other words, the sort of person who is destined to succeed.

In this final section I'm going to outline what to do with this amazing list of 100 goals that you've been working so hard to create throughout this program.

The short version is . . . go out and do them!

Simply get up, get out and begin playing the game of working each day toward checking each one of your goals off of your list.

Now, it really is that simple, but it doesn't mean that it's easy.

Simple is rarely easy.

But I want to make the attaining of your goals a good bit easier for you in the next hundred days so here's what I want you to do.

First, create several copies of your master goals list . . .

You'll need one for home, one for work and one to carry in your wallet or bag.

Ultimately, I want you to surround yourself with your goals wherever you are so that you're ALWAYS thinking about them.

Keep one copy in your bedroom by your bed and commit to reading it every morning when you first wake up and every night before you go to bed for the entire 100 days.

This is important as we're trying to teach your subconscious mind that these things are important to you, and the best way to do that is through repetition.

Next, check in on your MAGIC Hundred list AT LEAST twice a day while you're at work . . .

Why?

Because in the midst of the hustle and bustle of your daily life, it's easy to revert back to the behaviour, thoughts and feelings that have gotten you to where you are right now. That's fine if that's where you want to stay but if you're serious about moving forward then you really need to be vigilant about where your mind goes during the day.

I find it best to have the list up on the wall of my office, but do whatever works best for you, as long as you remember to do this.

I can't emphasise enough how important this is!

Next, I want you to **ask yourself a series of what I call** *daily power questions* first thing in the morning and last thing at night in order to both create and maintain momentum toward your goals.

In the morning

What THREE things can I do today to move me toward achieving my goals?

This can be answered in many ways. First, you may have an idea about something that you can achieve relatively easily in order to 'close a window' and clear mental space for other goals you may have a bigger goal that may require more time to achieve that will require daily effort on your part, or you may, as I often do, simply 'get a feeling' for the goal.

Often I'll just be sitting there looking over my MAGIC Hundred list and find that my eyes are drawn magnetically to one goal or another. This 'feeling' of what goal to aim for has rarely let me down, and I know many other MAGIC Hundred users that tell me the same thing.

You also need to ask *'Who can help me?'*

Coming back to our mastermind principle, you need to ask on a daily basis who you can get assistance from in order to meet your goal. This is because, as you move toward your goal, the level of assistance and the person who may be best able to assist may change. Asking this question daily then, serves to create a simple yet highly effective strategy for ensuring that you continue to get the help you need.

Next, you need to ask *'how will I feel when I achieve this?'*

Now, you may not be used to the idea of visualising, you may not even *believe* in it, but I'm going to ask you to suspend disbelief yet again and take 1 minute to visualise achieving each of your three goals and trying to actually imagine what it would be like to have them come to life for you.

At first you may feel strange and even a little silly. It'll pass.

Just spend that 60 seconds focusing on your goal and try to form a picture of what it'll look like, feel like, smell like and sound like when you actually achieve it.

Your brain doesn't know the difference between your imagined experiences and your real ones, so if you do this regularly enough, you'll be planting the seed of certainty that you *can*, will and *are* experiencing great success.

Finally, there's a section on your POWER Questions sheet for recurring goals. This is for things that may be ongoing over the hundred days rather than having a definite, finite target. For example, if you have a goal to drink 2 litres of water a day, walk for 20 minutes a day, read for 1 hour a day etc you may want to add them here.

Morning POWER Questions Sheet

What 3 Things Will I Do Today To Take Me Toward My Goals?	Who Can Help Me?	How Will I Feel When It's Complete?
1.		
2.		
3.		
Recurring Goals		

Evening POWER Questions Sheet

Did I achieve My 3 Goals?	Why Not?	Is There Still Time?
1.		
2.		
3.		
Recurring Goals		

Now to your evening questions.

These are three simply, yet extremely important self-checks that must be done every night for the entire 100 days.

First, ask yourself **'did I achieve the goals I set for today?'**

This allows you to assess if you're following up and keeping your word to yourself, the most important person in your life.

Obviously, some of your big goals are going to take a little time, you may not achieve them on the day you set them as they may be bigger and more difficult to attain in the short term. That's fine, but did you achieve the action step toward them?

If you did or if you went even further and actually completed the goal that you set for yourself, congratulations! Tick the goal off of your master sheet and take a moment to reflect on what it feels like to actually have another of your goals come true.

If no, then answer question 2.

Why Not?—Be honest here. You *must* be honest with yourself. If you didn't do it because you made an excuse then say so, if you ran out of time then say so, if you got distracted by other things then say so.

This is so important because if you can start to take responsibility for when things aren't working out so well then you can make changes to fix them. If you can't or if you try to justify or explain away your 'reasons why' then you'll forever be stuck blaming circumstances that you say are out of your control.

The final question is

Is there still time?

I've often gone to bed without having achieved my stated goals for the day. Quite often in fact.

As I lay in bed and go through my POWER questions, I often find that when I get to question three, the answer is *'yes, there IS still time'.*

Maybe I can pick up a phone and make a quick call, send an email, read that chapter, do those pushups or whatever else needs doing in order to take my action-step toward my goal.

The truth of the matter is, that barring real emergencies, there usually *is* still time and there's a *lot* we can do to not only stay on track but also to advance our goals and our lives dramatically.

That's what the MAGIC Hundred is all about really.

It's simply the day by day, step by step action that builds incredible momentum toward achieving the things we want from life, or as my mentor old Bob Proctor puts it *'The progressive realisation of worthy ideals'.*

It's an incredibly simple concept.

All it asks is that you follow some very straightforward principles like being clear about what you want, setting a plan of action, asking for help and consistently reminding yourself of what you want.

When put that way, it doesn't sound very magic at all does it?

Yet it really is.

The MAGIC Hundred has totally changed my life and the lives of many people that I have taught it to simply because its principles are those that are fundamentally rooted in truth.

As Jack Canfield, author of Chicken Soup for the Soul wrote of his own book *The Success Principles*, *'these principles will always work, as long as you work the principles'.*

What he means of course, is that you don't need to worry about whether or not what you've been taught will work.

It will. That is not in question.

There are thousands of people out there who have used this very program to become more successful and to develop greater happiness in their lives, proving to you, I or anyone interested enough to take notice, that what I've been describing to you WILL work.

So the question is not *'Will these principles work?'* but rather, *'will YOU work the principles?'*

Will you take the next 100 days of your life and put into practice faithfully, everything that you've learned in this programme?

Will you do it to the letter, without fail, every single day for 100 days?

If you do, you're assured of success. I guarantee it!

You see, this is simple cause and effect at work here. The principles you've been taught are the cause of success in all its forms.

In fact, no lasting success has ever been attained in any other way.

That being true, ONLY success can be achieved if you follow the principles right?

Once again, if this is alien to you and the seeds of doubt are pricking at the edges of your mind, I challenge you to suspend disbelief and do what every single successful person before you has done.

Act as if.

Act as if everything's a fun game.

Act as if you already have the things you want.

Act as if those you don't have are on their way to you.

Act as if the world is conspiring to do you good.

Act as if your success is guaranteed.

Act as if it is impossible to fail.

When you **act as if**, everything thing changes.

Therefore, when throughout this hundred day game that you're about to begin playing, it starts to feel all serious and like you're going to somehow fail and 'lose' in some way, simply act as if you're not.

In fact, act as if you *can't . . .* because you can't!

In parting, I'd just like to say thank you very much for letting me share the MAGIC Hundred with you and that I hope it brings you to everything you hope for yourself.

I know you have within you the power to achieve amazing things, we all do, I just sincerely hope that this time, this one time, you can actually complete the process of authoring and then living the life story that you really want instead of simply accepting the script that you've been given up to now.

You have the power to choose . . . use it!

Let's finish the book in the same way that we started . . .

The Fisherman's Tale
... a parable for a happy life

A businessman was on vacation in Mexico, taking a few weeks of well deserved R and R away from the hustle and bustle of his day to day life.

A passionate fisherman, one of the first things he did when he's plane touched down was to locate a company that ran deep sea fishing tours off the coast and arrange a fishing itinerary for the duration of the trip.

His very first enquiry brought him to the boat of an old fisherman who had obviously spent an entire lifetime at sea and, after just a few minutes in which the 2 connected with each other, he decided upon this boat and this man to be his guide for the whole of his stay.

During the vacation this chance paid off numerous times as the old captain seemed to always know the very best locations to visit at the best times of the day to ensure his passengers always got a least a few interesting bites.

By the end of the trip, the two had developed a free and easy manner of conversation and, as much as possible in so short a time, even considered it to be a friendship of sorts.

On the very last day, the businessmen turned to the old man and said *"Miguel, you really are the very best fishing tour operator I've ever met. Your knowledge of the weather, water, the fish, the boat and also the individual needs of your clients is amazing. You must let me help you to make this wonderful business of yours more successful"* he said'

"More successful?" asked the old man *"how"?*

"Well, for a start" went on the businessman *"I know a lot of people who would love to experience what I've experienced these last 2 weeks. I'm sure I could find a least 20 or 30 people. off the top of my head who would love to come and use your services"*

"But senor" Replied the old man *"I am but one person, I could not possibly look after so many!"*

"That's not a problem" the businessman *continued "with the profits from the first tours you could buy a second boat and crew to care for the new business you'd be attracting"*

"Then" the businessman went on, now obviously excited *"from the referrals you get from those people and a little strategic advertising you could buy more boats, hire more crews, and service even more people.*
Why, in 3-5 years you could be the biggest tour operator in this area. You'd be making millions!" 'He said triumphantly, obviously very pleased with himself.

The old man paused then asked *"but senor, why would I want to do all these thigs? What is the point of it all?"*

Baffled by the response the businessman said "The point is you'd be rich!"

"But what would I do with the money senor?" asked the old man.

"Do with it? why, you could do whatver you wanted. Just imagine, in 3-5 years time with some effort, you could have enough money to buy a beautiful house by the sea that you love so much, you could spend your days fishing, your nights entertaining family and friends and work only if and when you want to at whenever you choose . . . . You would be living the life of your dreams!" he was the businessman's reply.

The old man was silent, clearly mulling this new information over before he responded *"senor you are a good man and I know you mean well but these things you speak of are mine already.*

I live in the house that I have called home for more than 30 years with a wife that I love with all my heart and who loves me in return.

Every night I sit on the veranda with my wife and good friends, I watch the sun go down talk and laugh until it is time for bed.

At the weekend s my children and grandchildren visit and we make sandcastle on the beach, play and enjoy each other's company, and eat a meal together in the open air.

My work really isn't work to me.

I spend the day on the boat that I own free and clear, sailing waters I have know my whole life and guiding interesting and friendly people such as yourself to places I would gladly sail to far for my own pleasures, and I get paid a fair and generous sum for this.

I do not earn millions senor, yet I have all that you have described anyway. What need is there for me to create all of the extra work, the stresses and the strains to achieve in 3-5 years what I have right now?" He smiled.

It was the businessman's turn to be silent for a moment. Then he spoke

"I'm sorry my friend, I spoke out of turn. I thought I was teaching a simple man how to be successful when in truth it is you who have taught ME the secret of success . . ."

. . . Know what success looks like BEFORE you set out to find it!

Truth, joy and love

Dax

"I bargained with Life for a penny,
And Life would pay no more,
However I begged at evening
When I counted my scanty store.
For Life is a just employer,
He gives you what you ask,
But once you have set the wages,
Why, you must bear the task.
I worked for a menial's hire,
Only to learn, dismayed,
That any wage I had asked of Life,
Life would have willingly paid."

Napoleon Hill—Think and Grow Rich

What Now?

Don't think that just because you've come to the end of the book that there's nothing else to do. This isn't just one of those books where you read to the end, say *'that was nice'* and get on with your life.

As I've told you throughout the book, this is about doing, about ACTION!

> **If you haven't written your lists yet, then go back and do them now.**

> **If you haven't written your POWER Questions then they're next.**

Don't hang around, wait, think on it and then tell yourself that *you'll 'get around to it later'.*

In all likelihood, you won't.

Not because you don't want to, but because habit will re-assert itself and take over your life leaving you too tired, too distracted and too de-motivated to take action.

Do it now . . .

Do it NOW . . .

DO IT NOW!!

In fact, *'do it now'* needs to become your mantra over the next 100 days. Whenever you spot an opportunity to progress on one of your goals DO IT NOW is the order of the day.

I've made DO IT NOW a bit easier for you in the next few pages . . .

Your First Million!

I've decided to start your MAGIC Hundred Program off on the right foot by giving you your first million dollars.

No, this is not just some gimmick, this is a REAL exercise so pay attention.

Many people find the thought of earning a lot of money too abstract. They can't 'see' it which means that they find it hard to believe.

If you're one of those people, the physical act of seeing your million dollars in front of you every day for the hundred days might be all it takes to help you gain more focus and clarity for achieving your financial goals.

It worked for Jack Canfield and Jim Carrey and many others.

Why not you?

Cut this one out and keep it in your wallet.

Uh, uh, uh . . . . SUSPEND Dis . . . you got it!

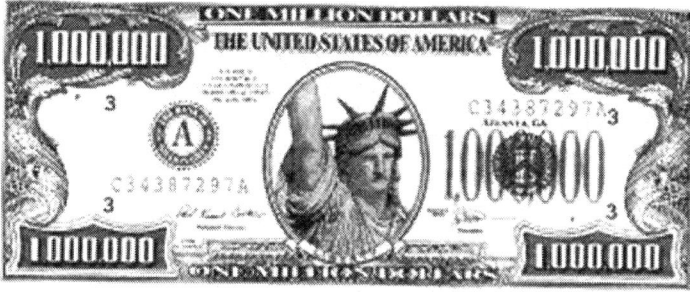

By the way, if you're not from the U.S. you can easily find your million note (whatever currency) by going to Google images and typing it in.

Try It For Your Home Too!

Best selling author of 'The Streetkids Guide To Having It All' and co-star of The Secret John Assaraf, tells of his vision board. A pinboard with photographs, sketches and newspaper clippings that helped him to visualise on the life he was trying to build for himself.

Upon that board he had a picture of a house. The house of his dreams that he focused intently on day in, day out for several years.

Well, as the story goes, John got a string of jobs that forced him to box his belongings up whilst he moved from place to place and build a career for himself.

After four years of constant upheaval, John finally settled down in a beautiful home in San Diego California. One day, whilst he was unpacking these boxes that had travelled with him over the years, his son pulled out one of John's vision boards and sent John into a state of shock.

Right there on the board were the car that John had always promised himself, the watch he told himself he'd buy and, amazingly, the house that was on his vision board. Not one *like* it, but the *exact* house!

Could this work for you?

Why not try it?

Build your own vision board and include as many pictures, sketches and photographs of what you want to have come into your life in the next hundred days.

Just build the board, look at it every day and imagine, really imagine, how you'd feel if you actually owned these things.

Wow!

"Nothing in the world can take the place of persistence.

Talent will not; nothing is more common than Unsuccessful men with talent.

Genius will not; unrewarded genius is almost a proverb.

Education will not; the world is full of educated derelicts.

Persistence and determination alone are omnipotent.

The slogan, 'press on' has solved, and always will solve, the problems of the human race."

Calvin Coolidge

Printed in Great Britain
by Amazon

81970385R00114